KARATEDO
ESOTERIC WISDOM

空手道
エソテリック
ウイズダム

KARATEDO ESOTERIC WISDOM

空手道 エソテリック ウイズダム

PROHIBITED KNOWLEDGE NOW DISCLOSED FOR THE FIRST TIME

KOUSAKU YOKOTA

横田耕作

To order additional copies of this book, contact:
Azami Press
1-765-242-7988
www.AzamiPress.com
Info@AzamiPress.com

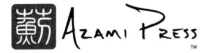

DEDICATION
奉納

I wish to dedicate this book to one of the most important gods in the Hindu pantheon, Shiva. According to *World History Encyclopedia*, Shiva "is considered a member of the holy trinity (trimurti) of Hinduism with Brahma and Vishnu. A complex character, he may represent goodness, benevolence and serve as the Protector. He is also associated with Time, and particularly as the destroyer and creator of all things" (www.worldhistory.org/shiva/).

The trinity of Shiva resembles the principles of *budo* karate. By mastering the skills of this art, a *karateka* can become a formidable protector. By protecting himself or someone else, he can become a destroyer of his enemies. By achieving the ultimate goal of karate, he can exhibit the last element of the trinity, which is benevolence and love. How fitting the representations of Shiva are!

KOUSAKU YOKOTA BIOGRAPHY
経歴

Shihan Kousaku Yokota (横田耕作), ninth *dan*, was born in 1947 in the city of Kobe, Japan, and has over sixty years of extensive martial-arts experience. Not only has he achieved mastery of Shotokan karate (with the JKA and under Master Asai), he has also studied other styles of karate, specifically Goju Ryu and Kyokushinkai. He is also familiar with the art of ki and judo and has experience with *kobudo*, as well, including nunchaku, *sai, tonfa, sansetsukon* (three-section staff), *nanasetsuben* (seven-section whip), and *kyusetsuben* (nine-section whip), in order to deepen and supplement his knowledge and skills in *karatedo*.

Yokota started his martial-arts training in 1957, when he was ten years old. He started taking lessons in judo at the Hyogo Prefecture police station, where he met a fellow student who also practiced karate but was practicing judo to further improve his fighting skills. Yokota was so impressed by him that, although he had been training in judo for three years, he made the decision to switch his training to karate. Yokota thus joined the Hyogo Prefecture Headquarters Dojo (兵庫県本部 道場) in Kobe and started his training in *karatedo* in 1961. He continued his karate training at the Kobe dojo until 1966, when he left for his university education in the U.S.A.

During his university years in the U.S.A. between the late sixties and early seventies, Yokota could not find a suitable dojo. He chose to train on his own until 1973, when he found the dojo of Master Teruyuki Okazaki (岡崎照幸, 1931 –2020), the founder of the International Shotokan Karate Federation (ISKF). Yokota moved to Philadelphia, PA, to become a full-time instructor at the headquarters dojo, as well as the personal assistant to the late Okazaki. Yokota was among the top competitors in the National and East Coast Regional Tournaments in the 1970s.

In 1981, he returned to his hometown of Kobe to complete his instructor training under the late Jun Sugano (菅野淳, 1928–2002), ninth *dan* and former vice chairman of the JKA. While in Japan, Yokota competed in the prefectural tournament and won the championship two years in a row. He represented his prefecture and competed in the JKA All Japan Championship in Tokyo in 1981 and 1982. He was also chosen as one of the prefectural representatives to the National Sports Festival (国民体育大会) in Shiga Prefecture in the fall of 1981.

After completing his JKA instructor training, Yokota moved to San Francisco, California, U.S.A., in 1983 to teach in Mountain View, CA. He received his fifth *dan* from the late Masatoshi Nakayama (中山正敏, 1913–1987) right before he passed away in 1987.

In 2001, he resigned from the JKA after forty years of membership to follow the late Master Asai in the Japan Karate Shoto Federation (JKS). Yokota received his sixth *dan* from Master Asai.

Master Asai passed away in 2006, and Yokota resigned from the JKS in 2009. He established his own organization, Asai Shotokan Association International (ASAI), in 2010 to promote his unique karate. He is the founder and worldwide chief instructor of ASAI as well as the president of the ASAI *shihankai* (師範会).

Yokota is also the author of six karate books: *Shotokan Myths* (Azami Press, 2010), *Shotokan Mysteries* (Azami Press, 2013), *Shotokan Transcendence* (Azami Press, 2015), *Karatedo Paradigm Shift* (Azami Press, 2017), *Karatedo Quantum Leap* (Azami Press, 2018), and *Karatedo Esoteric Wisdom* (Azami Press, 2022). He is seventy-five years old (as of July 2022). His age does not stop him from training more than four hours daily to maintain and improve his karate skills. Yokota also travels around the world to teach Asai Ryu karate and to promote *budo* karate to all karate practitioners who are interested.

ACKNOWLEDGMENTS
感謝の言葉

Many people are responsible for making the creation of this book, *Karatedo Esoteric Wisdom*, possible. I want to extend my gratitude to all those who have so generously contributed their time and experience to the creation of this book and to every person who purchases it.

In addition, I wish to express my special appreciation to one Japanese karate master who seems to be connected to me in a strange and invisible way. He has

assisted and guided me in the search of true *karatedo*. His name is Yuji Kamihara (神原祐司), and he is from Nagoya, Aichi Prefecture. Let me present his background and his impressive qualifications.

Shihan Kamihara has been practicing Shotokan karate for sixty years as he started his karate training in the JKA in 1962. He entered the Shotokai in 1965 because the karate club at his university, Nanzan University (南山大学), belonged to the Nihon Karatedo Shotokai (日本空手道松濤會). For this reason, his karate was influenced by Shigeru Egami, the founder of the Shotokai. He is also a researcher and his lifetime endeavor is to find the relationship between *kata* and *bunkai*.

He is currently the chairman of the Kokusai Karatedo Shoto Nankukai (国際空手道松濤南空會) and holds the rank of eighth *dan* in this organization. He also serves as a member of the *shihankai* of my organization, ASAI. Due to his mastery of *karatedo*, ASAI presented its first ninth-*dan* diploma to him in 2017. His other *dan* ranks include seventh *dan* in the Zenjitsuren, seventh *dan* in the Gakuren, sixth *dan* in the All Japan Karatedo Shotokan (AJKS), and third *dan* in the Zenkuren (JKF).

Let me explain why I want to mention him in this book. After the passing of Master Tetsuhiko Asai in 2006, I was somewhat lost. After my resignation from both the JKA and the JKS, only a few of my karate associates in Japan wanted to maintain our friendship. I was a ronin. The few who maintained their relationship with me were not my seniors, nor were they more knowledgeable in karate.

About eight years ago, by chance, I came to know Shihan Kamihara through a popular Internet site. Almost instantly, we became very close associates, and he later became my best karate friend, though this sentiment may not be reciprocated. For all these years, we have exchanged our ideas and opinions on many different subjects related to karate. We have agreed on most things, but sometimes we have had different ideas. We have welcomed this as we have been able to learn from these different ideas.

He also invited me to give a seminar in Japan. I had given many seminars around the world, but no Japanese person or organization had invited me before. My first seminar in Japan became possible in 2018. I was so happy that I could finally share my knowledge of Asai karate and its techniques in Japan. There were quite a few participants, not only from his organization but from others, as well, including other styles. I think it was a successful event thanks to him.

Shihan Kamihara was generous enough to invite me again. Unfortunately, I have not been able to do so due to the worldwide pandemic situation. I hope I will be able to do so in the near future.

The biggest contribution I received from him may be that he taught me the importance of investigation and research into karate history. Until that time, I had not considered history that much and did not think it was that important. He made me see that I was wrong. To understand the current state of karate, you must know its history to see how it changed and how the past had an impact on modern-day karate. I really want to thank Shihan Kamihara from the bottom of my heart.

In the end, I want to thank every *karateka* in the world. I want to emphasize that true enjoyment of karate resides in practicing it physically and also mentally. The true essence of the martial arts is stated in the term *shingitai* (心技体), and this is exactly what is missing from modern-day karate. I consider this essence to be the true esoteric wisdom.

FOREWORD

By Chong Tong Long (Paul Chong)

Godan, Asai Ryu

Chairman, Taiwan Karate Association Development Association

Country Representative, ASAI Taiwan

Kaohsiung, Taiwan

欣聞橫田耕作老師又有新作！ 此書是揭露空手道武道本質的智慧與奧秘。其內容表現出空手道一些秘傳智慧此誠為可喜可貴。 空手道源自古老的東方，它蘊藏著無限的人體奧秘與心靈智慧！ 空手道是武道！它不是表面一般所看到所理解的拳打腳踢！ 它在人體工學的運作下一個表面 看似無奇的動作卻可產生極大的威力！ 並且超越年齡的局限！ 然而在當今競技比賽盛行的情況下，空手道的人口雖越來越多，技術訓練卻越偏於打點取分式的練習。 空手道固有的奧秘、本質、多元性的本質已越來越趨於式微。 一般教練大都沉醉於比賽用的那些招法卻忽略了武道本質的空手道多元豐富內涵，此實在是遺珠之憾。 橫田老師是少數執著於武道修煉不惑於時下流行的競技空手道的老師，其本人更是學養深厚絕佳的武者。 今天他這部「空手道深奧的智慧」的問世，提出了人們漸漸忘記或該說忽略掉武術奧秘的內容，希望有志此道的學者勿等閑視之。

English

I'm glad to hear that Kousaku Yokota Sensei's newest book is coming out! This book unveils the essential wisdom and mystery of karate. The content imparts the invaluable secret wisdom of karate. The origin of karate is in the Ancient East, and it contains unlimited secrets of the human body, as well as the wisdom of the mind!

Karate is *budo*! It is not just fighting techniques. It works beneath the layer of ergonomics. Seemingly simple moves can actually carry extraordinary power. Karate also goes beyond the restrictions of age. However, with sports and games becoming more prevalent in modern society, and even with the increasing number of karate practitioners, karate training ends up focusing on scoring and winning the competition. The original secrets, essence, and plurality of karate has eroded as a result.

It is such a shame that most karate teachers immerse themselves in the techniques best suited for competition but fail to remember how rich and diverse the essence of karate is. Kousaku Yokota Sensei is one of the few that insist on *budo* training and haven't succumbed to the latest trend in competition-oriented karate.

Kousaku Yokota Sensei himself is an excellent and learned *bushi*. Today, his work, entitled *Karatedo Esoteric Wisdom*, points out how the modern world gradually forgets, or, more accurately, loses sight of the secrets of the martial arts and calls on like-minded scholars to not lose sight, either.

Foreword

Nicolaos Nicolaides

Yondan, Asai Ryu

Country Representative, ASAI Cyprus

Limassol, Cyprus

Ο Shihan Kousaku Yokota έχει ένα πλούσιο βιογραφικό το οποίο συμπεριλαμβάνει την συγγραφή έξι βιβλίων και παρά πολλών άρθρων με κύριο θέμα τους το καράτε και γενικότερα τις πολεμικές τέχνες. Το συγγραφικό του έργο, φυσικά, αντιπροσωπεύει την τεράστια του εμπειρία όσο αφορά το καράτε αφού ο ίδιος το μελετά, προπονείται σε αυτό και το διδάσκει για δεκαετίες τώρα. Η συσσώρευση όλης αυτής της γνώσης και σοφίας καταγράφεται στα βιβλία του όπως και στο παρόν βιβλίο *Karatedo Esoteric Wisdom*.

Πέραν, όμως, της τεράστιας εμπειρίας του Shihan Kousaku Yokota, των γνώσεων και ικανοτήτων του, αυτό που χαρακτηρίζει τα βιβλία του και τα καθίστα ξεχωριστά είναι το γεγονός ότι περιέχουν πληροφορίες που δεν υπάρχουν αλλού. Επίσης, τολμά να αμφισβητήσει τις καθιερωμένες θεωρίες και αρχές, βλέποντας πέραν του φανερού, του κοινότυπου και του συνηθισμένου.

Όλα τα πιο πάνω είμαι σε θέση να τα επιβεβαιώσω αφού έχω μελετήσει όλα τα βιβλία και άρθρα του. Το παρόν βιβλίο δεν αποτελεί εξαίρεση. Σε αυτό εξετάζει και αναλύει πολλά ενδιαφέροντα θέματα με τον δικό του μοναδικό και ιδιόρρυθμο τρόπο προσφέροντας στον αναγνώστη, πέραν της θεωρίας, πραγματικές και πρακτικές γνώσεις τις οποίες μπορεί να χρησιμοποιήσει κατά την προπόνηση του αλλά και στην καθημερινή του ζωή. Έξαλλου, γι' αυτό είναι *karatedo* δηλαδή 'ο τρόπος ζωής του Καράτε'!

Το καράτε δεν είναι απλώς ένα άθλημα. Πρωτίστως είναι πολεμική τέχνη, επιστήμη, φιλοσοφία, η ίδια η ζωή. Ο Shihan Kousaku Yokota το γνωρίζει πολύ καλά αυτό και μας μεταφέρει με μαεστρία στον θαυμαστό κόσμο του καράτε.

Ο τίτλος του βιβλίου *Karatedo Esoteric Wisdom* εκφράζεται πλήρως στις σελίδες του βιβλίου και ο κάθε καρατέκα, και όχι μόνο, όταν το διαβάσει σίγουρα θα είναι κατά πολύ σοφότερος!

English

Shihan Kousaku Yokota has a rich biography that includes the writing of six books and many articles focusing on karate and martial arts in general. His written work, of course, represents his vast experience in karate since he studies it, trains in it, and has been teaching it for decades now. The accumulation of all this knowledge and wisdom is recorded in his other books as well as in this book, *Karatedo Esoteric Wisdom*.

But, beyond Shihan Kousaku Yokota's vast experience, knowledge, and skills, what sets his books apart is the fact that they contain information that no other book has. He also dares to challenge established theories and principles, looking beyond the obvious, the commonplace, and the ordinary.

I am able to confirm all of the above since I have studied all his books and articles. This book is no exception. In it, he examines and analyzes many interesting topics in his own unique and peculiar way, offering the reader, in addition to theory, real and practical knowledge that he can use not only in his training but also in his daily life. After all, that's why it is called *karatedo*, i.e., 'the karate way of life'!

Karate is not just a sport. It is primarily a martial art, science, philosophy, life itself. Shihan Kousaku Yokota knows this very well and takes us with mastery to the wonderful world of karate.

The title of the book, *Karatedo Esoteric Wisdom*, is fully expressed in the pages of this book, and, after reading it, every *karateka* will surely be much wiser!

FOREWORD

By Ali Baheri Oskui

Rokudan, Shotokan

Country Representative, ASAI Iran

Osku, Iran

بی تردید کتاب کاراته دو حکمت باطنی حضرت عالی حاصل سالها تلاش شما در راستای اهداف استاد گیچین فوناکوشی و استاد تتسو هیکو آسای بوده و از آنجا که یکی از اهداف بزرگ کاراته اتحاد روح و جسم در کاراته سنتی و انسان ساز است لذا آموزه های این کتاب که خواننده را به سوی کمال ابدی و عشق جاودانی که در نهایت تمرین در کاراته سنتی پدیدار میشود هدایت می کند امید آن دارم که این کتاب مورد مطالعه جامعه کاراته قرار گیرد و بهره کافی را از اندیشه های شما ببرند

English

Your karate book, *Karatedo Esoteric Wisdom*, has undoubtedly been the product of your many years of effort toward the goals of Master Gichin Funakoshi and Master Tetsuhiko Asai. Since one of the great goals of karate is the union of body and soul in traditional and man-made karate, the teachings of this book guide the reader toward eternal perfection and eternal love and, finally, practice in traditional karate. I hope this book will be studied by the karate community and that they will benefit from your ideas.

FOREWORD

By Evgeny Raspertov
Rokudan, Asai Ryu
Country Representative, ASAI Russia
Moskow, Russia

В книге "Каратэдо Эзотерическая мудрость" Шихан Йокота собрал огромное количество информации, касающейся философских, кинезиологических и фундаментальных аспектов пути каратэ и боевых искусств.

Информация, которую вы найдете, никогда ранее не раскрывалась ни одним из многочисленных авторов книг о боевых искусствах, а также не преподавалась на занятиях по каратэдо.

Эта книга – книга для размышлений, а не прямой ответ. Главы 7 и 8 наведёт вас на мысли правильно ли вы осмысляли своё кумитэ, а также о сложившейся соревновательной системе многих организаций.

Поначалу вас озадачит то, с чем вы будете знакомиться в этой книге, возможно этот материал собьёт с толку или даст основание к новым мыслям о правильности того, что вы делаете на тренировках.

Глава 4 возможно расскажет Вам об истинном значении слова умереть. Как умирают оставаясь при этом живым и как избежать этого.

Читая эту книгу, в конце концов, вы обнаружите, что информация чрезвычайно проницательна, которую можно найти только в учении Шихана Йокоты.

Такие темы как «Тайна Ирими» или «Истинное значение каратэ начинается с Уке» могут быть немного сложны для понимания новичков, но я уверен, что это очень познавательно и поучительно для опытных мастеров боевых искусств.

Глава 12 была для меня открытием по практике дыхательных упражнений, улучшению общего самочувствия и выносливости человека. Что важно для всех возрастов каратэка.

Затронутые темы могут побудить многих читателей задуматься о глубине их знаний в Будо или о том, чему их учили. Они также будут побуждать их к дальнейшему переосмыслению или изучению своего понимания и мотивировать их расширять свои знания, смотреть не только на лицевую сторону монеты.

Шихан Йокота пытается сказать нам, что изучать каратэ - это не просто практика физических движений, но и нечто большее, что раскрывается в его книге. Мы также должны попытаться понять и уважать его философию, которая так же важна, если не больше, как технические навыки. Он призывает нас постоянно бросать вызов самим себе умственно и интеллектуально.

English

In the book *Karatedo Esoteric Wisdom*, Shihan Yokota has collected an enormous amount of information around philosophy, kinesiology, and fundamental aspects of karate and martial arts.

Information you might find has never been brought to light by any of the numerous authors of martial-arts books, and this was not taught during *karatedo* classes.

This book is a book for thinking and asking rather than for providing answers. Chapters 7 and 8 will lead you to challenge your own understanding of *kumite* as well as the competition setting across many organizations.

At first, you'll be puzzled by this book's contents. Perhaps this material may trick you or even plant seeds to drastically change your way of thinking about what is actually right in your practice during classes.

Chapter 4 may tell you about the true meaning of the word *die*, how to die while staying alive and how to avoid it.

At the end of the day, while reading this book, you will discover how precise the information is and how unique and exclusive it is to the studies of Shihan Yokota.

Topics such as the mystery of *irimi* or how the true meaning of karate starts with an *uke* may seem confusing to beginners, but I'm confident that they are very educational and enlightening for seasoned martial artists.

Chapter 12 was a revelation for me on the practice of breathing exercises, improving one's general well-being and endurance, which is important for *karateka* of all ages.

The topics touched on here may make you reflect on the depth of your knowledge of *budo* or what you have been taught. And, they will continue to make you think differently, reinvent your understanding, motivate you, expand your knowledge, and, at last, form a deep and thorough mindset.

Shihan Yokota is telling us that karate practice is not just physical exercise. It is so much more, which is highlighted in the book. At the same time, as readers, we are to understand and respect his philosophy, which can be even more important than technical skill. This is the call to challenge ourselves, both mentally and intellectually.

Foreword

By Fabio Alfonso Ávila Gómez

Yondan, Asai Ryu

President, ASAI Colombia & Director, ALAC

Bogotá, Colombia

Karatedo Esoteric Wisdom hace parte del profundo estudio del *karatedo* y los hallazgos que ha realizado Shihan Kousaku Yokota durante todos sus años de experiencia. Ésta es una obra de obligatorio conocimiento para cualquier *karateka* si quiere aprender a comprender las enseñanzas que, a través de la práctica diaria, nos muestra el *karatedo*.

En ocasiones, esas enseñanzas son directas, y, en otras más comunes, debe analizarse detenidamente lo que se hace ya que es por medio del ejercicio que se llega a la sabiduría esotérica.

El resultado de la práctica de una técnica perfectamente ejecutada se traduce en el perfeccionamiento de acciones cotidianas que, aparentemente, nada tienen que ver con el *karatedo* pero que se benefician de él.

La obra es un recorrido por todos los elementos que comprende practicar el *karatedo* y es, además, una exposición de lo que se ve y lo que no se ve. Estos últimos elementos, los que no se ven, son los que, de alguna manera, determinan la formación del artista marcial.

Yo recomiendo ampliamente este libro ya que, en lenguage sencillo y con ideas innovadoras, nos hace ver que hay aspectos de nuestro *karatedo* que están ahí. Los vivimos y sencillamente no los vemos ya que no los relacionamos con el arte marcial.

El *karatedo* está en todo, y todo es el *karatedo*.

English

Karatedo Esoteric Wisdom is part of the deep study of *karatedo* and the findings that Shihan Kousaku Yokota has made during all his years of experience. This is a work of compulsory knowledge for any *karateka* if he wants to learn to understand the teachings that *karatedo* shows us through daily practice.

Sometimes those teachings are direct, and, on other, more common occasions, what is done must be carefully analyzed since it is through exercise that esoteric wisdom is reached.

The result of the practice of a perfectly executed technique translates into the improvement of daily actions that, seemingly, have nothing to do with *karatedo* but benefit from it.

The work is a journey through all the elements involved in practicing *karatedo* and is also an exhibition of what is seen and what is not seen. These last elements, those that are not seen, are the ones that somehow determine the formation of the martial artist.

I highly recommend this book since, in simple language and with innovative ideas, it makes us see that there are aspects of our *karatedo* that are there. We live them and simply do not see them since we do not relate them to the martial art.

Karatedo is in everything, and everything is *karatedo*.

PREFACE
初めに

Higi

I am truly happy to see my sixth book being published this year. To my surprise, it has been four years since I published the last one, *Karatedo Quantum Leap*, in 2018. Believe it or not, it was fairly easy for me to complete the previous five books. I honestly enjoyed writing them and making the knowledge come out in print.

When I wrote the material for those books, the ideas often just popped up into my mind. It was like a spring where the water flows out nonstop from nowhere. It was almost as if someone were in my head, telling me what to write. Physically, all I had to do was just type what I "heard." You may not believe it, but, in many parts of the books, it was just like that. Therefore, I thought my sixth book would also be easy. In fact, I was planning to publish another book in 2020.

Unfortunately, that did not happen. In late 2019, I lost my touch. The spring seemed to have stopped its flow. When I sat down to write, it was almost painful to come up with ideas. I struggled to complete each chapter. There were many chapters that were only half or partially done, and I could not complete them. I think I know the reasons, but, regardless, this limbo period lasted all throughout 2020 and 2021. Then, in early 2022, I am happy to say that, for the first time in over two years, I got my motivation back. I was finally able to complete the unfinished chapters.

So, let me explain the title of this book. Many readers might not consider the word *esoteric* to fit with *karatedo*. When you say something is esoteric, people tend to assume it is mystical or spiritual or maybe even strange or weird. I am aware of this, but I decided to use this term as I believe it is appropriate. Let me explain.

First, let's look up the definition of this word. The broad definition of esoteric is given in *Merriam-Webster's Collegiate Dictionary, Eleventh Edition*, as "difficult to understand" and also as "of special, rare, or unusual interest." This is no surprise; however, the fine definition I want to share with you is this: "requiring or exhibiting knowledge that is restricted to a small group." This definition is exactly why I chose this word. The ideas and information you will find in this book were

understood and possessed by only a small group of *karateka*. These few enlight-
ened *karateka* would rather keep their wisdom and knowledge than share it with
the public. I am trying to bridge the gap and help those who are seeking enlightenment or simply the answers to their questions.

I sincerely hope this book will give you not only new and unique discoveries
but also much excitement and happiness.

Contents

CHAPTER ONE
第一章

SHIVA, LORD OF THE DANCE
シバ神一踊りの神

According to the *Encyclopædia Britannica*, Shiva means 'Auspicious One' in Sanskrit. He is one of the main deities of Hinduism, and Shaivites worship him as the supreme god.

The mythology of Shiva is quite long and involved, but here is a summary of it just to give you a general understanding of what Shiva represents:

> Shiva is represented in a variety of forms: in a pacific mood with his consort Parvati and son Skanda, as the cosmic dancer (Nataraja), as a naked ascetic, as a mendicant beggar, as a yogi, as a Dalit (formerly called untouchable) accompanied by a dog (Bhairava), and as the androgynous union of Shiva and his consort in one body, half-male and half-female (Ardhanarishvara). He is both the great ascetic and the master of fertility, and he is the master of both poison and medicine, through his ambivalent power over snakes. As Lord of Cattle (Pashupata), he is the benevolent herdsman—or, at times, the merciless slaughterer of the "beasts" that are the human souls in his care. Although some of the combinations of roles may be explained by Shiva's identification with earlier mythological figures, they arise primarily from a tendency in Hinduism to see complementary qualities in a single ambiguous figure.

It goes on to say as follows:

> Shiva is usually depicted in painting and sculpture as white (from the ashes of corpses that are smeared on his body) with a blue neck (from holding in his throat the poison that emerged at the churning of the cosmic ocean, which threatened to destroy the world), his hair arranged in a coil of matted locks (*jatamakuta*) and adorned with the crescent moon and the Ganges (according to legend, he brought the Ganges River to earth from the sky, where she is the Milky Way, by allowing the river to trickle through his hair, thus breaking her fall). Shiva has three eyes, the third eye bestowing inward vision but capable of burning destruction when focused outward. He wears a garland of skulls and a serpent around his neck and carries in his two (sometimes four) hands a deerskin, a trident, a small hand drum, or a club with a skull at the end. That skull identifies Shiva as a Kapalika ("Skull-Bearer") and refers to a time

when he cut off the fifth head of Brahma. The head stuck to his hand until he reached Varanasi (now in Uttar Pradesh, India), a city sacred to Shiva. It then fell away, and a shrine for the cleansing of all sins, known as Kapala-mochana ("The Releasing of the Skull"), was later established in the place where it landed. (www.britannica.com/topic/Shiva)

The reason I decided to write about Shiva was the fact that he is also called *Nataraja*, which means 'Lord of the Dance' in Sanskrit. I again turn to the *Encyclopædia Britannica* for a brief description of this Hindu mythology, where we find that Nataraja is

the Hindu god Shiva in his form as the cosmic dancer, represented in metal or stone in many Shaivite temples, particularly in South India.

In the most common type of image, Shiva is shown with four arms and flying locks dancing on the figure of a dwarf, who is sometimes identified as Apasmara (a symbol of human ignorance; *apasmara* means "forgetfulness" or "heedlessness"). Shiva's back right hand holds the *damaru* (hourglass-shaped drum); the front right hand is in the *abhaya* mudra (the "fear-not" gesture, made by holding the palm outward with fingers pointing up); the back left hand carries Agni (fire) in a vessel or in the palm of the hand; and the front left hand is held across his chest in the *gajahasta* (elephant-trunk) pose, with wrist limp and fingers pointed downward toward the uplifted left foot. The locks of Shiva's hair stand out in several strands interspersed with flowers, a skull, a crescent moon, and the figure of Ganga (the Ganges River personified as a goddess). His figure is encircled by a ring of flames, the *prabhamandala*. In classic Sanskrit treatises on dance, this form, the most common representation of Nataraja, is called the *bhujungatrasa* ("trembling of the snake").

It further states that

the gestures of the dance represent Shiva's five activities (*panchakritya*): creation (symbolized by the drum), protection (by the "fear-not" pose of the hand), destruction (by the fire), embodiment (by the foot planted on the ground), and release (by the foot held aloft). (www.britannica.com/topic/Nataraja)

According to the *Wikipedia* article on Nataraja,

the two most common forms of Shiva's dance are the *Lasya* (the gentle form of dance), associated with the creation of the world, and the *Tandava* (the vigorous form of dance), associated with the destruction of weary worldviews—weary perspectives and lifestyles. In essence, the *Lasya* and the *Tandava* are just two aspects of Shiva's nature; for he destroys in order to create, tearing down to build again. (en.wikipedia. org/wiki/Nataraja)

Here are some other important and interesting points that can be found in that same *Wikipedia* article:

- He dances within a circular or cyclically closed arch of flames (*prabha mandala*), which symbolically represent the cosmic fire that in Hindu cosmology creates everything and consumes everything, in cyclic existence or cycle of life. The fire also represents the evils, dangers, heat, warmth, light and joys of daily life. The arch of fire emerges from two *makara* (mythical water beasts) on each end.
- He looks calm, even through the continuous chain of creation and destruction that maintains the universe, which shows the supreme tranquility of the Atma.
- His legs are bent, which suggests an energetic dance. His long, matted tresses, are shown to be loose and flying out in thin strands during the dance, spread into a fan behind his head, because of the wildness and ecstasy of the dance.
- On his right side, meshed in with one of the flying strands of his hair near his forehead, is typically the river Ganges personified as a goddess, from the Hindu mythology where the danger of a mighty river is creatively tied to a calm river for the regeneration of life.

- His headdress often features a human skull (symbol of mortality), a crescent moon and a flower identified as that of the entheogenic plant *Datura metel*.
- Four-armed figures are most typical, but ten-armed forms are also found from various places and periods, for example the Badami Caves and Ankor Wat.
- The upper right hand holds a small drum shaped like an hourglass that is called a *damaru* in Sanskrit. A specific hand gesture (mudra) called *damaru-hasta* (Sanskrit for '*damaru*-hand') is used to hold the drum. It symbolizes rhythm and time.
- The upper left hand contains *Agni* or fire, which signifies forces of creation and destruction. The opposing concepts show the counterpoise nature of life.
- A cobra uncoils from his lower right forearm, while his palm shows the *Abhaya* mudra (meaning 'fearlessness' in Sanskrit), suggesting not to fear nearby evil, as well as evil and ignorance surrounding the devotee as he or she follows the righteousness of *dharma*.
- The lower left hand is bent downwards at the wrist with the palm facing inward, we also note that this arm crosses Naṭarāja's chest, concealing his heart from view. It represents *tirodhana*, which means 'occlusion', 'concealment'.
- The face shows two eyes plus a slightly open third on the forehead, which symbolize the triune in Shaivism. The eyes represent the sun, the moon and the third has been interpreted as the inner eye, or symbol of knowledge (*jnana*), urging the viewer to seek the inner wisdom, self-realization. The three eyes alternatively symbolize an equilibrium of the three Gunas: Sattva, Rajas and Tamas.
- The dwarf upon whom Nataraja dances is the demon *Apasmara purusha* (Muyalaka, as he is known in Tamil), and who symbolizes the demonic evil and ignorance over which the sacred dance of Shiva gives victory.
- The slightly smiling face of Shiva represents his calmness despite being immersed in the contrasting forces of universe and his energetic dance.

The above interpretations of symbolism are largely based on historic Indian texts published in and after the twelfth century.

Below are some excerpts from a Khan Academy article on Shiva that was written by Farisa Khalid:

A Dance within the Cosmic Circle of Fire

Here, Shiva embodies those perfect physical qualities as he is frozen in the moment of his dance within the cosmic circle of fire that is the simultaneous and continuous creation and destruction of the universe. The ring of fire that surrounds the figure is the encapsulated cosmos of mass, time, and space, whose endless cycle of annihilation and regeneration moves in tune to the beat of Shiva's drum and the rhythm of his steps.

Beyond Grace There Is Perfection

The supple and expressive quality of the dancing Shiva is one of the touchstones of South Asian, and indeed, world sculpture. When the French sculptor Auguste Rodin saw some photographs of the 11th century bronze *Shiva Nataraja* in the Madras Museum around 1915, he wrote that it seemed to him the "perfect expression of rhythmic movement in the world." In an essay he wrote that was published in 1921 he wrote that the *Shiva Nataraja* has "what many people cannot see—the unknown depths, the core of life. There is grace in elegance, but beyond grace there is perfec-

tion." The English philosopher Aldous Huxley said in an interview in 1961 that the Hindu image of god as a dancer is unlike anything he had seen in Western art. "We don't have anything that approaches the symbolism of this work of art, which is both cosmic and psychological."

The eloquent bronze statue of the *Shiva Nataraja*, despite the impact of its formal beauty on Rodin who knew little of its background, is incomplete without an understanding of its symbolism and religious significance. Bronzes of the Chola period such as *Shiva as Lord of the Dance (Nataraja)* arose out of a need to transmute the divine into a physical embodiment of beauty. (www. khanacademy.org/humanities/ap-art-history/south-east-se-asia/india-art/a/shiva-as-lord-of-the-dance-nataraja)

Conclusion

I have taken up much space to provide
this information so that the reader will have
a general idea about the god Shiva and the
meaning of his divine dance. I think the story is
incredibly interesting, and I can understand the
French sculptor Rodin's impression that this is
the "perfect expression of rhythmic movement
in the world." I also agree with the English phi-

losopher Aldous Huxley (1894–1963), who said in an interview over sixty years
ago that "we don't have anything that approaches the symbolism of this work of
art, which is both cosmic and psychological."

The more I look at this statue and its design, the
more I start to think about Busaganashi, the martial
art god of Goju Ryu (剛柔流). From what I had
read about Busanagashi in several articles, mostly in
Japanese, Goju Ryu practitioners have few hypotheses regarding the source. In other words, we do not
really know what the origin of this image is, and, in
the end, no one is sure if any of these ideas are true.

If you are interested in reading more on this subject, there is an excellent article
by Andreas Quast on the *Ryukyu Bugei* website entitled "Heroes and Gods: The
Factual Existence of a Transmission of Ethical Teachings and Practical Philosophy in Karate, Exemplified by the God of War Būsāganashī ブーサーガナシー."
Here is the link: https://ryukyu-bugei.com/?p=7767.

After considering the shape of these figures and also learning about what
Shiva represents, I suspect the origin of Busaganashi could be the divine Lord
of the Dance, Shiva. This may be a wonderful discovery not only for Goju Ryu
practitioners but also for all karate practitioners around the world. Do you agree
with my suspicion, or is this only my wishful thinking?

CHAPTER TWO
第二章

WHY IS THERE A STATUE OF SHIVA AT CERN?
シバ神とセルンの関係とは？

After I completed the previous chapter, I came across a very interesting fact. There is a statue of Shiva at CERN, which is home to the Large Hadron Collider and is one of the premier research institutes in the  world. In fact, this two-meter-tall statue of the dancing Shiva was presented by the Indian government to CERN in 2004.

When I discovered this, I became very curious about the relationship between these two entities, and I needed to find out why this happened. What was or is the relationship between Shiva, a Hindu deity of India, and this European center for research in particle physics in Switzerland? An interesting question, isn't it?

Initially, these two things did not seem to go together, at least to me. Thus, I needed to go deeper to find the relationship as the answer to this question might shed light on a possible reason this premier research institute received a statue of Shiva.

 I already gave an explanation of Shiva in my previous chapter, so I will start this chapter with my research on what CERN is all about. If you hear the name *CERN*, you may recall its large-scale collider. We need to find out more about this institution to explain its relationship to Shiva.

In short, CERN is the European Organization for Nuclear Research, although its acronym stands for *Conseil européen pour la recherche nucléaire*. In fact, it operates the largest particle-physics laboratory in the world. Established in 1954, the organization is based in a northwest suburb of Geneva, Switzerland, and has twenty-three member states.

CERN's mission can be found on its website (home.cern): "At CERN, we probe the fundamental structure of the particles that make up everything around us. We do so using the world's largest and most complex scientific instruments." These instruments include the Large Hadron Collider (LHC). The website states that the LHC is the most powerful particle accelerator in the world. A test magnet reached a peak magnetic field of 13.5 teslas. The tesla (T) is the unit

used to measure the strength of magnetic fields, and one tesla is equal to 10,000 gauss (G). The experiment facility is a giant circular tunnel of superconducting magnets with a number of accelerating structures to boost the energy of the particles along the way. The tunnel is about 17 miles (27 kilometers) long and is positioned between 165 and 575 feet (50 and 175 meters) below the ground. It started up in September 2008.

If you wish to learn more about the collider, check this URL: home.cern/science/accelerators/large-hadron-collider.

In the previous chapter, we learned that the statue of Shiva symbolizes his cosmic dance of creation and destruction. Now we discover that the research center was created to probe the fundamental structure of particles. Maybe we are getting some hints about the relationship between these two. One interesting fact is that the Indian government presented the statue of Shiva to CERN to celebrate the research center's long association with India. Very interesting. Now we need to look at the history of the Indian government's involvement with CERN.

According to CERN's website,

India and CERN signed a Cooperation Agreement in 1991, setting priorities for scientific and technical cooperation, followed by the signature of several Protocols. India's relationship with the Organization dates back much further, initially through cooperation with the Tata Institute of Fundamental Research, whose high-energy physicists have been actively participating in experiments at CERN since the 1960s. They were later joined by scientists from the Raja Ramanna Centre for Advanced

Technology, Indore, in the 1990s. These and other institutes built components for the LEP accelerator and the L3, WA93 and WA89 detectors. Their scientists participated in important physics analyses and publications throughout the years.

All these developments paved the way, in 1996, for the Indian AEC (Atomic Energy Commission) to agree to take part in the construction of the LHC, and to contribute to the CMS and ALICE experiments and to the LHC Computing Grid with Tier-2 centres in Mumbai and Kolkata. In recognition of these substantial contributions, India was granted Observer status to the CERN Council in 2002. (home.cern/news/news/cern/india-becomes-associate-member-state-cern)

Now I can see the heavy involvement of the Indian physicists at CERN. Obviously, for this reason, the Indian government decided to present a gift to the institute in 2004. This might have resulted in India's becoming an Associate Member of CERN in 2017. This is a big achievement for India, and I am happy to learn this. At the same time, I still needed to find out why the gift had to be a statue of Shiva. The Indian government could have presented something else that was very Indian, such as a statue of an elephant or a model of the Taj Mahal. Why did it have to be Shiva? Was it by chance or on purpose?

There is a special plaque next to the presented statue, and this may give us a hint as to the significance of the metaphor of Shiva's cosmic dance. The plaque is engraved with a quotation by Fritjof Capra (1939–). Who is this guy? Most of us

may not know him even though he is a famous scientist. He is an Austrian-born American physicist and systems theorist. You may remember the title of his book, *The Tao of Physics* (Shambhala, 1975). This book was pretty popular in the late seventies and into the eighties. Even I, an amateur in science, have heard the title before. I find the subtitle of the book, *An Exploration of the Parallels between Modern Physics and Eastern Mysticism*, to be very interesting as it implies a bridge between two separate worlds. In this book, he claims that both physics and metaphysics mysteriously arrive at the same knowledge.

Here is the entire quote from the plaque:

Hundreds of years ago, Indian artists created visual images of dancing Shivas in a beautiful series of bronzes. In our time, physicists have used the most advanced technology to portray the patterns of the cosmic dance. The metaphor of the cosmic dance thus unifies ancient mythology, religious art and modern physics.

Isn't this interesting? Capra also gives the following explanation in his book:

The Dance of Shiva symbolizes the basis of all existence. At the same time, Shiva reminds us that the manifold forms in the world are not fundamental, but illusory and ever-changing. Modern physics has shown that the rhythm of creation and destruction is not only manifest in the turn of the seasons and in the birth and death of all living creatures, but is also the very essence of inorganic matter.

He further states,

According to quantum field theory, the dance of creation and destruction is the basis of the very existence of matter. Modern physics has thus revealed that every sub-atomic particle not only performs an energy dance, but also is an energy dance; a pulsating process of creation and destruction. For the modern physicists then, Shiva's dance is the dance of subatomic matter, the basis of all existence and of all-natural phenomena.

Wow! What do you think? The quote below is an interesting reflection on the statue by Aidan Randle-Conde, a young scientist who worked at CERN:

So, in the light of day, when CERN is teeming with life, Shiva seems playful, reminding us that the universe is constantly

The Dance of Shiva and Sub Atomic Particles

Shiva statue at Cern (Shiva was the first Yoga teacher) and the LHC (Large Hadron Collider) at CERN Particle Physics Lab in Switzerland.

shaking things up, remaking itself and is never static. But by night, when we have more time to contemplate the deeper questions, Shiva literally casts a long shadow over our work, a bit like the shadows on Plato's cave. Shiva reminds me that we still don't know the answer to one of the biggest questions presented by the universe and that every time we collide the beams, we must take the cosmic balance sheet into account.

The late Carl Sagan (1934–1996) was the one who introduced this idea in the West through his TV show *Cosmos*. He had the following to say:

> The Hindu religion is the only one of the world's great faiths dedicated to the idea that the Cosmos itself undergoes an immense, indeed an infinite, number of deaths and rebirths. It is the only religion in which the time scales correspond, no doubt by accident, to those of modern scientific cosmology. Its cycles run from our ordinary day and night to a day and night of Brahma, 8.64 billion years long, longer than the age of the Earth or the Sun and about half the time since the Big Bang. And there are much longer time scales still.

Interestingly, not everyone was happy with the statue of Shiva at CERN. The institute has been accused of playing God by conservative Christians, particularly when they identified the Higgs boson in 2012 and it was named after physicist Peter Higgs (1929–). In 2013, Higgs and François Englert (1932–) were awarded the Nobel Prize for their theoretical predictions. In the mainstream media, the Higgs boson has often been called the *God particle*. However, this nickname is strongly disliked by many physicists, including Higgs himself. Some accused CERN, saying that this statue represents a destroyer. CERN management tried to justify having the statue based on the fact that India was one of the institute's Observer states (which was true) and that this represented CERN's multiculturalism. I can tell management tried very hard.

Let me finish this chapter with a quote by Aldous Huxley, an English writer and philosopher who wrote nearly fifty books. Huxley stated the following:

When you think of the staggering symbols that the
Indians produced—I mean, the Dancing Shiva, for
example—we've never produced anything as comprehensive as this. The Dancing Shiva—those little bronze
statues—it is the Shiva with four arms dancing with
one foot raised. And, well, I mean, I go into the details.
They're really quite extraordinary.

Here is the link to his 1961 interview in Lon-
don where he mentions Shiva: www.youtube.com/
watch?v=32oo0oyLUdE. It is about seven minutes
long and interesting to listen to.

The statue shows Shiva performing the Tandava, which is a dance that is
believed to be the source of the cycle of creation, preservation, and destruction.
I know CERN's experiments are intended to create its own small "big bang" or
"creation." Will this bring us a key to preservation? Or, will it have a negative effect that may lead the world to its destruction? Does anyone know the true intention of CERN and the real reason the statue of Shiva was placed there?

CHAPTER THREE
第三章

THE MYSTERY OF THE VISIBLE AND THE INVISIBLE
可視と不可視の不思議

When I was very young, I used to believe that only what I could perceive with
the senses of my body, such as my vision, hearing, touch, etc., was real and nothing else. As I grew, I learned about different scientific disciplines, such as physics, chemistry, astronomy, etc. I remember the big shock I felt when I learned
about light. The term *light* typically refers to visible light, which is, in fact, electromagnetic radiation that can be detected by the human eye. The electromagnetic
spectrum consists of electromagnetic
waves ranging from way below
1 hertz to above 1025 hertz. One
important fact is that visible light is a
band that ranges from approximately
405 to 790 terahertz.

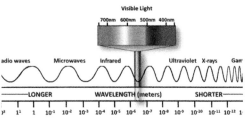

When I learned these facts, they certainly did not shock me simply because
I did not understand what they really meant. However, when I discovered what
they represented, it definitely shuttered my belief that only what was visible was
all there was around us. Would you believe that the band of visible light represents only 0.0035% of the entire electromagnetic spectrum? You can find this
data in the article "Visible Light" on the National Nuclear Security Administra-
tion (NNSA) website (www.energy.gov/nnsa/articles/visible-light-eye-opening-
research-nnsa). They give this percentage and state that "the entire rainbow
of radiation observable to the human eye only makes up a tiny portion of the
electromagnetic spectrum."

I am aware that some readers may be thinking, *I thought this book was about
karate. I don't understand why this author is talking about this*. I understand this
doubt, but let me continue for a while longer, and I will relate this to karate later.

OK, the realization of how limited we are in our vision made me think further, and I began to see—no pun intended—more invisible things that we are surrounded by. For instance, even though there is a segment of the population that
does not believe in God, according to a review on atheism by sociologists Ariela
Keysar and Juhem Navarro-Rivera, 7% of the world's population is registered as

positive atheists and agnostics.

That is a very interesting fact. But, at the same time, this means 93%, or the majority of the world population, believes in God. Isn't God invisible? Yet, we believe in God. The ultimate teach-

ing of most religions is love. If you have your own children, I am sure you love them. Love is invisible, so it is difficult to show. So, we buy presents, we say, "I love you," and we do nice things to express our love. Money is something you can see and something many people consider to be very important. However, if I asked you if you would marry someone you didn't love for money, I am pretty sure you would say no. Most of us would marry a man or woman who was poor if we fell in love with that person. Why? It is simply because most of us consider love, which is invisible, to be more important than money, which is visible.

As I looked around, I discovered the world of yin and yang in this world. According to an article by Jun Shan on the *ThoughtCo.* website (www.thoughtco. com/yin-and-yang-629214), the meaning of this ancient Asian concept is that "the universe is governed by a cosmic duality, sets of two opposing and complementing principles or cosmic energies that can be observed in nature."

If you look around, you will see many examples of this kind of thing, such as day and night, an active state and a passive state, heat and cold, fire and water, being awake and being asleep, the sun and moon, etc.

What I was most intrigued by was the yin and yang of the visible and the invisible. Even though invisible things are not necessarily more important than visible things, I find that many people believe this is the case simply because these things are invisible, such as spiritual beliefs. For me, these two elements are of equal importance, and it cannot be one-sided.

Some people do not share my belief, and I would like to share one example here. When I was young, I was a salesman in the USA. My boss used to tell me, "It does not matter how you get an order. The only thing that counts in your performance is the dollar amount of the orders you get." In other words, he was hinting at two things. One was that I could possibly lie or bribe to get an order. Another was that the amount of effort I put in did not count at all. In other words, no matter how hard I worked, I would be a failure if I could not get an order. The order and the dollar figure were visible things. Lying, bribing, and working hard were invisible things. What was important to my boss was only the visible things. I never made a good salesman, and I was proud of it.

Whether invisible elements are always more important or not, I must say that they are often ignored or de-emphasized. I can say this is also true in karate training, and this leads me to the main topic of how this is all related to karate.

Let's think about karate techniques. Even though there are many different kinds of techniques, we typically say karate skill consists of punches and kicks. For a punch, you use your arm and fist. These are the visible elements. Even the punch itself is a visible element. A kick is the same. You use your leg and hit with your foot. You can see all these parts as well as the action of the kick. No problem there.

For a punch, your arms move, and for a kick, it's your legs. But, how do they move? Of course they're moved by the muscles that are in those limbs. Those muscles are there, and you know this intellectually, but you cannot see them. Let's dive further. How do the muscles move? Your brain has to send a signal to the muscles. Your arms and legs are connected to your brain via an intricate network within your nervous system. The nervous system is a physical element, so you can see it if you look at an anatomical chart. However, it is only a conductor through which your brain has to send an electrical impulse. This impulse is more or less invisible. However, you can connect your body to some kind of measuring equipment, and, by doing this, you may be able to see the impulse in the form of waves.

Then, we need to ask, "How does this command to move the arm or leg occur?" It is the will or desire you have in your head. That is where it starts, but where can we find this will or desire? It is totally invisible, isn't it? Can we then say that something invisible controls something visible? That is interesting but is not that important. We have to ask the next question. Where does that will or desire come from?

One well-known French philosopher and scientist of the seventeenth century, René Descartes, wanted to know what we are. He left us the famous quote "*Cogito, ergo sum*" ('I think, therefore I am'). It is true that we think, and so we are. But, I bet he could not tell us where the ideas or concepts came from when he thought. Some medical scientists are now saying that the

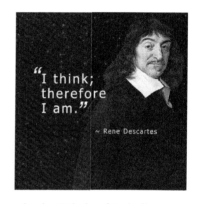

memories and concepts we have do not reside in our brain. It is hard to believe, but they propose that memories and concepts may be stored outside the brain. They explain that it is similar to the computer systems we currently have. The amount of data that resides inside a laptop is small. The vast majority of the information is stored in a cloud or on the network itself. I am not 100% sure if this hypothesis is correct or not, but I think it is very interesting. If you are interested in this subject and willing to pay for the full content, you can read the article "Can Memory Exist outside of Brain and Be Transferred? Historical Review, Issues & Ways Forward," which can be found in the *Medical Hypotheses* journal on the *ScienceDirect* website: www.sciencedirect.com/science/article/abs/pii/S0306987717304553.

You may wonder why I am talking about this. What is the relationship between this and karate? Well, this is because I wish to bring up the sensitive subject of ki (気). In your karate training, many sensei may tell you, "Bring your ki together," or, "Strengthen your ki." You hear it is important, but what is ki? Even though you have heard this word many times before, many readers are not exactly sure what it is.

It is difficult to define or explain this mysterious concept, isn't it? I wrote about it in Chapter 7: "What Is Ki?" of my book *Shotokan Transcendence*. If you are interested in this subject, you can get a copy of this book and find a detailed explanation there. In general, I consider ki to be a universal energy that gives and sustains life. In other words, this is the energy source that controls the mental and spiritual side of our body (as opposed to the physical side).

On the physical side, we eat, drink, and breathe to gain energy for our body to live. Air provides oxygen to our lungs. By going through the digestive system, water and food provide necessary nutrition and glycogen, the energy source. These necessities are circulated to every part of our body through a comprehensive network of blood vessels. Through this system, we are able to stay healthy and to have the energy to move our body. This is not a mystery, and all of us know this.

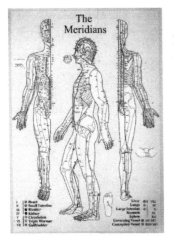

The Meridians

How about the invisible side, though? Did you know that we have a network of ki within our body? It is made up of *keiraku* (経絡, 'meridians'). A chart showing such a network is called a *meridian diagram* (illustration left). It indicates that an intricate network of ki channels seems to exist within our body. In fact, acupuncturists use this type of diagram to know the special points for treatment. Are the meridians and the points visible? No, they are not. However, acupuncture treatment has proven to be effective and sometimes even better than modern-day medicines or medical treatment. So, there must be something there to substantiate the positive results.

It is said that ki flows through our body via this meridian network. As the ki circulates throughout our body, it finds some key points or terminals. There are three major terminals that are called *tanden* (丹田) in Japanese and *chakra* in the practice of yoga. These three *tanden* are very important in all martial arts and in other traditional Japanese arts, as well, which include Zen meditation. I wrote about the *tanden* in Chapter 12: "There Is More Than One Tanden" of my book *Karatedo Paradigm Shift*.

Even though the *getanden* (下丹田, 'lower *tanden*'), also known as the *seika tanden* (臍下丹田, 'lower abdominal *tanden*'), is the most valued in martial arts, including karate, I believe all three are equally important. As this chapter is not focused on the *tanden* itself, I will skip this explanation. I suggest you get ahold of the book I mentioned above and read that chapter for further discussion on this

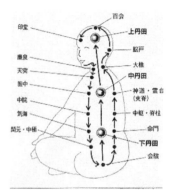

subject. The point I want to make here is that invisible things, such as ki or the *tanden*, are very important in karate. Yet, they are very difficult to understand and even more challenging to develop, improve, and strengthen.

If you want to improve your karate skill, it is definitely important and necessary to train physically. Flexibility, balance, and muscle strength are all important. You should repeat a *kata* (形) a thousand times or more. You should also indulge in *kihon* (基本, 'basics') training to sharpen particular techniques. However, I say that doing all of that is not enough. I have seen so many practitioners spend hours sweating and exhausting themselves, but their karate skill was not impressive. Why is this so? What is missing?

My humble opinion is that they are training their body too much. Many readers may be shocked, or even offended, by this statement. Believe it or not, if you practice incorrectly, the more time you spend, the worse you become. It is a sad statement, but it is also a sad truth. In addition, by not using your body correctly, you could damage yourself, namely, your knees, hip joints, etc. I have seen so many senior practitioners who have had to undergo knee or hip-joint surgery. Some of them had to quit training. Would you not agree that karate training should never harm your body? If this is so, why do so many practitioners damage their joints? They did not listen to their body.

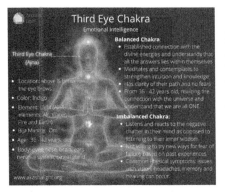

Third Eye Chakra
Emotional Intelligence

How can you listen to your body? It is simple once you learn how to do it. In short, you need to develop an internal "eye" and "ear." Armed with those tools, you should feel what your body tells you. How do you develop an internal eye and ear? Of course I am not suggesting that you would develop a real organ in the form of an eye or an ear. Rather, I am referring to the ability to perform the functions of an eye and an ear. Of course, this ability is invisible as it is similar to the sense of feeling.

Then, how can you develop this ability or sense? The answer to this question is rather easy. You can do this by simply doing nothing or almost anything. One popular method is, believe it or not, meditation. Here we must pay our respects to the wisdom of Zen Buddhists. They could spend their time and devotion only on praying and chanting the holy scripts. As you know, they spend many hours in Zen meditation, during which they just sit down and try to think about nothing. Instead of doing something, they choose to do nothing or almost nothing. Is it not a wonderful reflection of yin and yang?

OK, you will say, "I understand that Buddhist monks want to meditate as they desire to achieve enlightenment. However, we *karateka* are different. We are not looking for enlightenment. We want to improve our physical ability to perform karate techniques. Explain why you are talking about this."

This would be a reasonable request if we were not seeking enlightenment. However, I would like to explain that we are trying to achieve enlightenment through karate training. In Zen Buddhism, they may be searching for spiritual enlightenment. In karate, we need to reach the same goal using our physical movements. The biggest difference is not that it is physical. Rather, it is that we also need to combine the physical (visible) with both the mental and the spiritual (invisible).

Interestingly, in ancient China, the Buddhist monks realized that spiritual endowment alone was not sufficient. By spending all day chanting, they became weak and sickly. Thus, they created the physical exercise *qìgōng*, or *kiko* (気功) in Japanese. They added this set of exercises to their daily routine in addition to their religious rituals. These physical exercises consisted of controlling their breathing system

as they slowly moved the limbs of their body to improve their health. In the late fifth or early sixth century, this eventually developed into an empty-hand fighting system called *Tai Ji Quan* (太極拳 [*tàijíquán*]), a style of kung fu that is more commonly known simply as *tai chi*.

I am not proposing that you include chanting or religious activities in your training. One of the things I am proposing is that you invest more effort in emptying your mind rather than focusing on the physical aspects of karate techniques. You need to be able to think and feel as you execute each technique. This is why I recommend that you practice slowly, or at least more slowly. I respect tai chi. Many readers know that this is the style in which almost all the movements are done extremely slowly. This process allows practitioners to think and feel each technique. They can pay attention to all of their body parts (both inside and outside) in order to move in the best form.

In many dojo, we have a lineup ritual at the beginning and also at the end of training. This is, of course, to show respect to the instructor by bowing. However, you are probably aware that a short *mokuso* (黙想, 'meditation') is part of the ritual. This is not by accident. The objective of the *mokuso* before class is to forget about worldly worries and concerns, such as money, work, relationship problems, etc. The objective of the *mokuso* at the end of class is to keep the empty mind that you developed during training so you can carry it into your life outside the dojo.

Master Gichin Funakoshi (船越義珍, 1868–1957), the
founder of modern-day karate, left us his famous *Niju Kun*
(二十訓, 'Twenty Principles'). Each one of the principles
is meaningful and educational, but one of them applies
directly to the subject we are discussing here. The fifth principle is *gijutsu yori shinjutsu* (技術より心術). *Gijutsu* (技
術) literally means 'technique', but here he was referring to
physical karate techniques. *Yori* (より) is a word that shows
that what comes before it is lesser than what comes after it
(here referring to its relative importance). *Shinjutsu* (心術)

is a rare term that consists of the characters *shin* (心), meaning 'mind' or 'heart',
and *jutsu* (術), meaning 'technique', 'method', or 'art'. When put together,
shinjutsu means 'mental technique' or 'mental method'. So, he was saying mental
technique was more important than physical technique. Isn't that interesting? I
truly agree with his teaching here.

You may be wondering what he meant by "mental technique." As far as I
know, he did not leave any explanation or detail as to what exactly a mental
technique was. He might have explained it verbally in one of the classes he gave,
but we can only guess at this time. Some people say it was the positive attitude
of the practitioner, a never-give-up attitude that is popular in Japan. Others say
it was a feeling of *zanshin* (残心, 'remaining mind'). By having *zanshin*, you
place a large sensory dome around you that will alert you if any danger enters.
Still, others say he might have been referring to etiquette. In other words, a karate
practitioner must be courteous and polite.

Any one of these ideas may be correct. The most important point of Funakoshi's teaching, which I would like to emphasize, is that he placed mental technique above physical technique. I would like to expand this subject a little further
to illustrate that karate should be practiced according to the concept of yin and
yang.

We live in the twenty-first century, and our life is constantly surrounded by computers. Almost everyone in the world has at least a computer, if not a smart-phone. We see and use the computer's or the phone's hardware. In other words, we talk, communicate, listen to music, view videos, etc., through these devices. We almost worship the convenience of this toy or tool. However, if you under-stand even a little about how a computer or a smartphone works, you know that the hardware is a dumb terminal and that what is really important is the software inside it. Yes, memory size is important, but the ultimate importance belongs to the applications and programs that reside inside the hardware.

There is, interestingly, some similarity in the concepts of computer capability and karate skill. For instance, if you know many *kata* or techniques, you can say you have many apps on your computer. If you practice something deeply, such as a *kata*, then you can say you have sophisticated software. If you train incor-rectly and acquire bad habits, then this is like having bugs in your software. Even though I am not a computer engineer, I know that the capability of a computer depends on both its hardware and its software. The following statement may be debatable, but it is commonly understood that the invisible part, which is the capability of the software, is more important than the visible part, which refers to things such as the screen, the keyboard, the disk drive, and even the chips. I think it is interesting to find a parallel here.

Let us go back to the hardware and software of the body and look at how they work when you try to improve your karate skill. Of course, the hardware part is easy as this is the body. On the other hand, what is the software part? Some people may say it is the brain. However, the brain itself is also a piece of hardware because it is something that contains software, which is the knowledge and skill sets it possesses. When you are born, you, of course, have a brain. At the same time, this brain is almost empty and needs to learn many things. A baby's brain, however, is not quite empty. A baby is born with instinct, knowledge that does not need to be taught. A baby knows how to cry, how to suck on a nipple to drink milk, etc. In addition, all of the physical functions, such as respiration, digestion, and excretion, preexist and are naturally functional.

Karate techniques must be learned just as you need to learn how to walk, talk, ride a bike, etc. Most people learn how to walk and talk unless they have a physical handicap. On the other hand, there are some who cannot ride a bike, swim, ski, skate, or drive a car. These skills or abilities are not essential to live. They require interest and motivation. You must spend some time, weeks or months, to acquire them.

Skills such as riding a bike or driving a car require time to learn, but it takes only a few weeks to acquire such skills. After a few months, you can even learn how to ski or skate. Of course, it will take many years of training if you wish to be an expert swimmer or skier who can compete in a regional or national competition, though.

When it comes to an expert level of karate skill, seemingly, it is far more challenging. In fact, only a small part of the population can attain such a level. It is said that only one in a hundred white belts is able to reach a black-belt level. It used to be one in a thousand in the last century. Due to commercialism and sport karate's wide popularity, more people can attain (or buy) a black belt these days.

Regardless, first-degree black belt, *shodan* (初段), is commonly understood to be the beginning level of serious karate training, not the expert level. You would have to be at least a fourth degree, *yondan* (四段), before you could be classified as a karate expert.

So, how long does it take to get to fourth degree? First of all, you need to train at least two or three years to make it to first degree. After that, you need to train diligently—a minimum of three nights per week—for at least another ten years. You can pass the *yondan* exam if you are in good shape. In our organization, Asai Shotokan Association International (ASAI), a *yondan* candidate must take a written exam before the physical exam. A challenging subject is given to the candidate, and he must write an essay of six to ten pages based only on his own knowledge and experience (without cutting and pasting information from the Internet).

Learning is an interesting but complex topic. I will not go into this subject in this chapter because I wrote about it in Chapter 16: "Moving the Body vs. Using the Body" of my book *Karatedo Quantum Leap*, where I share my understanding of the mechanism of learning in detail. If you are interested in this subject, you can get a copy from *Amazon*.

Finally, I want to touch on another challenging subject about the invisible side, which has to do with the mental and spiritual aspects. Both are invisible and are critical for karate training. But, before we go into the details of each aspect, I must bring up some interesting facts.

One fact is that many karate practitioners consider these two aspects to be the same. In other words, they believe that the mental aspect and the spiritual aspect refer to the same thing. This is because, for them, the meaning of the word *spiritual* has to do with either being in high spirits, which refers to joy or happiness, or having a fighting spirit, which refers to an aggressive or combative attitude. They simply consider such spiritual feelings and attitudes to have mental origins or require mental involvement.

Many other practitioners believe there is no room in karate for spirituality, which refers to the human spirit or soul as opposed to physical or material things. In other words, the spirituality of karate is not related to the Shinto (神道) religion. This is, I suppose, because many non-Japanese practitioners in the Americas and in Europe are Christian, Jewish, or Muslim. It is amazing that many dojo located outside Japan imitate the traditional Japanese dojo by including a Shinto shrine, but no one seems to care about it or make a big deal about it. On the contrary, they consider it to be "cool" and accept it as something very traditional.

A funny thing, at least to me, I find in many dojo is that they build a *torii* (鳥居). And, in some, it's even built with the shrine inside the dojo. A *torii* is a Shinto gate or entrance that leads to a shrine. I am sure their intention is not religious. Their actions possibly come from accidental ignorance or a pure misunderstanding as they believe the *torii* is related only to karate or Japanese martial arts and unrelated to the Shinto religion. Most dojo in Japan have a *kamidana* (神棚), which is a portable Shinto shrine. However, I have never seen a *torii* in any of the dojo in Japan, though I have visited many dozens of them.

I consider the mental and spiritual aspects of karate to be different. I will explain how they differ, but, before I proceed with the explanation, I want to emphasize that this is only my personal opinion. It may be quite different from yours. I expect some readers may feel uncomfortable or disagree with the idea. I only ask that you keep an open mind and step outside the box a little just to see things from a different perspective as this can be mentally stimulating.

The mental aspect of karate has to do with the things that come from our consciousness. This, of course, requires the involvement of the cerebrum, which is the part of our brain that consists of a left and right hemisphere. According to Johns Hopkins Medicine, the cerebrum is the largest part of the brain, and it

> initiates and coordinates movement and regulates temperature. Other areas of the cerebrum enable speech, judgment, thinking and reasoning, problem-solving, emotions and learning. Other functions relate to vision, hearing, touch and other senses. (www. hopkinsmedicine.org/health/conditions-and-diseases/anatomy-of-the-brain)

In addition, and particularly important for our discussion, it is known that the cerebrum is also responsible for general motor skills, while the cerebellum, located behind the brain stem, is responsible for fine motor skills. According to SSMHealth,

> while the frontal lobe controls movement, the cerebellum "fine-tunes" this movement. This area of the brain is responsible for fine motor movement, balance, and the brain's ability to determine limb position. A stroke in this area of the brain can lead to paralysis or "jerky" muscle movements. (www.ssmhealth.com/neurosciences/stroke/brain-anatomy)

So, anything having to do with learning or the functions of body movement within the art of karate is, in my estimation, all mental. I do not think there is any issue with this statement. Of course, within the mental aspect, interestingly, we find both visible and invisible components, but we will not go into the details of that here. I am sure the reader can figure this out with just a small amount of research.

The challenging part of our discussion is the spiritual aspect of karate training. It is true that the word *spirit* is often used during the karate training I have observed in Western English-speaking countries. An instructor may say, "Give it some spirit!" or, "Show some spirit!" He is asking for a loud or louder *kiai* (気合). In other words, he is talking about fighting spirit. I think a loud *kiai* or showing this kind of spirit is fine for sport karate or youth training. I wrote about this in Chapter 5: "Silent Kiai" of my book *Shotokan Myths*. In short, you let out a loud *kiai* when you are a beginner. As you become advanced, though, you need to grow into the stage of the silent *kiai* or soundless *kiai*.

OK, so when I use the words *spirit* or *spiritual*, I am not referring to a fighting spirit or a battle-ready mentality. I am talking more about a higher self or a religious state. I am aware that I am now touching on a subject that is debatable and also very sensitive. I may be the only karate instructor who dares to discuss this matter. I do this because I sincerely believe this is a critical requirement, yet it is missed in almost all karate training.

Discussing this subject in this context may be quite rare in the Western world. However, I need to share that it is not so rare in Japan. In fact, for some serious Japanese practitioners of any *budo* (武道, 'martial art'), including karate, training itself is a religious matter. This may be a surprising statement for some readers. But, with some investigation, you will realize that this is not anything strange or unique.

If you are involved in kenjutsu (剣術), iaido (居合道), kyudo (弓道), or any other ancient Japanese ancient *budo*, you might have witnessed a Shinto ritual being performed at some important event, such as a New Year dojo opening or a national demonstration. In most modern-day karate, unfortunately, the Shinto ritual has been omitted or de-emphasized, mainly due to commercialism.

Despite this, if you are still not convinced regarding the relationship between martial arts and religion, consider the link that can be found in kung fu. You have most likely seen the kung fu workout routine of the monks of the famous Shaolin Temple in China. There-

fore, what I am presenting here is not a far-fetched idea. On the contrary, it is a hidden truth in Japanese *budo*, including karate. I am aware that the subject of religion is a touchy and very sensitive one. Many readers may not feel comfortable or may disagree with the idea I am presenting here. All I am asking is that you open your mind and just read until the end. At the end, you are free to accept or reject the concept presented here. I hope you will not make up your mind before reaching the end of this chapter.

Does this mean that a *budo* practitioner must convert to Shinto or Buddhism? No, not at all. If you believe in God or the Creator of Christianity, Islam, or any other religion, that is where you can start. What I am trying to say is that the

word *spirit* as used in the martial arts refers to
the achievement of enlightenment. Achieving
such a phenomenon requires both physical and
metaphysical training. This is why yoga practitioners talk about opening seven chakras through
their training. In Zen, the Buddhists choose to
do it through clearing the mind in seated meditation. At the Shaolin Temple, the daily duties are a
combination of sutra chanting and kung fu training.

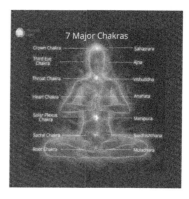

Shintoism is worshiping nature and the creator of the universe. It is a type of
animism, and it respects all the religions of the world. Japanese culture is unique
in that it opens the door to all religions as we believe that all of the gods or things
that are worshipped come from the same source. As I mentioned earlier, karate
training does not require you to change your religion. What I am proposing here
is that in order to reach the ultimate level of understanding karate and its skill set,
it is necessary to achieve spiritual enlightenment. The level I am referring to is
not a standard expert level. Almost anyone can reach that level by practicing hard
for many years. There is an exceptional expert level, a one-in-a-million kind of
expertise. Those who reach this level are known as *tatsujin* (達人) in Japanese.
This is the level I am referring to.

To reach this level, you must clear an invisible barrier. It seems difficult, but
I am confident it can be achieved if you understand how. Of course, I have not
reached this level yet, but I can share what I have learned so far from my own
research and training. I may know the exact path, but I cannot reach that level
unless I take that path to the summit. I am still on the way, so I can show you the
path I have taken so far. Here is what I think is needed in karate training.

First of all, we must examine the context of spiritual enlightenment. My
understanding is that the goal is to achieve an ability beyond our five senses. This
refers to senses that are supposed to exist but that the average person does not
possess. Sensing the invisible vibrations around us is one example of a key abil-

ity that is beyond our five senses. This invisible vibration can be called *ki*.

In the written record of the seventeenth and eighteenth centuries, we see this superhuman ability often exhibited by famous samurai (侍) such as Musashi Miyamoto (宮本武蔵, c. 1584–1645 [illustration left]) and Munenori Yagyu (柳生宗矩, 1571–1646). I will not go into the details of what happened here as I have already written about it to some extent in my previous works. This incredible ability was also depicted in the movie *Seven Samurai*, (七人の侍 [Toho Studios, 1954]), directed by Akira Kurosawa (黒澤明, 1910–1998). In the scene in question, a samurai who is about to enter an inn detects another samurai who is hiding behind a door, ready to strike the person with a wooden sword if he enters.

Initially, you need to train to feel the vibration, or ki, of another person. Then, you can expand to other things, eventually getting all the way to the point of feeling the ki of the earth. There may be a ki of the universe, but I will stop at the realm of the earth for the purposes of this discussion.

So, how do we train to feel the ki of another person? One way that comes to mind is team *kata* training. Some senior karate practitioners write off team *kata* as mere synchronized dancing. I agree that the very effort to perform *kata* techniques in a synchronized manner takes a big chunk out of the meaning of the techniques as these should be performed according to the timing and rhythm of your imaginary opponent. In other words, if you have to speed up or slow down for reasons other than what would feel comfortable or correct if the *kata* were performed alone, then that *kata* must be considered ineffective or poorly performed. This may be very true from that perspective.

Having said that, I would like to present a different idea from another perspective. How about if the hidden objective of team *kata* is to feel the ki of the other performers or to develop an invisible connection with them? I am sure you have seen the ability of certain birds, such as blackbirds, starlings, shorebirds, and robins, to fly together as a unit, twisting and turning as though the whole flock were one bird. It is incredible to see how they can change direction instantly. It is amazing to witness hundreds of starlings flying together in a whirling and constantly changing pattern.

You also know that certain fish, such as herring, anchovy, and even tuna, congregate together as a tight group. This is called *shoaling*. They swim in the same direction at the same speed in a coordinated manner, and they turn in unity as though the whole group, or school, were one fish. Their actions are instantaneous as though they were wired together. Maybe they are magnetically connected, but I do not know exactly how. I know that a fish in the back cannot see the fish in the very front. It always amazes me when I watch a school of anchovy in an aquarium demonstrate such an ability.

There may be other animals that possess the same ability to defend themselves. I am pretty confident that the evolutionary humans of many thousands of years ago, who were some of the weakest mammals, must have had an innate talent for detecting danger and acting as a group in a consorted manner. It must be one of the instincts that have been long forgotten or stored away in our brain. What if we could bring this back if trained? I do not think this is impossible or even unrealistic. We have witnessed people gain extraordinary hearing abilities when they lose their vision.

And, we do not even need to go that far to experience something similar.

Have you ever experienced a feeling that you are being watched and then discovered as you turned around that someone was watching you from behind or from the side? I hear that women exhibit this ability more strongly than men. Isn't this an instinct that still exists? Though this instinct is also disappearing, it can be strengthened by sharpening the mind. I am sure you will agree that martial-arts training is an effective training method.

Quantum physics now says that human consciousness determines reality.

In other words, only when we see something does it exist. It may be difficult to understand this concept, but they say that if no one watches the moon, then it does not exist. Quantum physics also tells us that a single photon behaves like both a wave and a particle, which is called *wave-particle duality*. We face two contradictory pictures of reality when we try to explain the phenomenon of light. It determines its particular properties when it is observed, and the side of the dual properties that manifests itself will depend on how we observe it.

If you wish to better understand this subject, you can read the article "Duality Principle Is 'Safe and Sound'" by David Barnstone: https://www.rochester.edu/newscenter/duality-principle-is-safe-and-sound-researchers-clear-up-apparent-violation-of-quantum-mechanics-wave-particle-duality/.

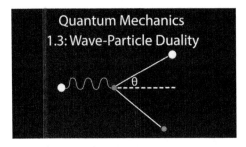

OK, we are not going to go into the details of photons and photon experiments here. I just wanted to bring up these scientific facts to show that we cannot say something does not exist just because we cannot see it. In other words, reality is much broader and more complex than we expect or realize in our daily life.

So, back to team *kata* training. When I was competing in tournaments in the seventies and eighties, I competed not only in individual *kumite* (組手, 'sparring') and *kata* but also in team *kata*. After practicing with the same teammates every week for a few years, I began to feel something unique while practicing *kata* day in and day out. It is difficult to explain. It was a kind of light sensation, a feeling of magnetic connection. In other words, each member was on the same invisible track and had the same rhythm so that we could move in unity almost without even trying. I could almost see my teammates behind me. If they were slightly behind or not up to the speed, I would slow down. If they were ahead of me, I would speed up a little to make the adjustment. I shared my feelings with my teammates, and they admitted that they had also experienced a similar feeling.

When we were in good condition, our team moved almost like one person. It was almost like a school of fish or a flock of birds. We thought we were almost perfect. At the Hyogo Prefecture Championship (兵庫県大会) in 1982, in the last competition we participated in, we thought we could take first place. To our disappointment, we came in second. We performed Jutte (十手), and the team beat us performed Unsu (雲手). I really believe we did better than they did. The *kata* they performed was more attractive, and they probably looked better. Even though we did not take first place, I learned something very important. I felt I could expand myself outside the visible sphere.

I go into this subject a little more deeply in Chapter 4: "What Is the True Objective of Team Kata" of my book *Karatedo Quantum Leap*. You can read this chapter if you are interested in the subject. You may agree that you can develop this feeling or the ability to connect to the members of your *kata* team. But, then you may say, "So what? How would that apply to the essence of karate or self-defense?"

That question is fair and reasonable. If you can extend your senses or ki feelings to your teammates, maybe you are able to do this to anyone around you. Wouldn't this ability help you when you are out in public, especially if you are alone at night?

As I am a *budo* practitioner, I am not interested in competitions, but this ability can be beneficial. If you happen to be a sport-karate *kumite* competitor, wouldn't it be a great advantage if you could sense your opponent's next move?

I believe this sense is one of our lost instincts. Many thousands of years ago, when we had to live in more dangerous environments without any modern-day equipment or tools, we had to depend on our inner abilities. Lacking certain abilities was a matter of life or death. Of course, physical strength and agility, both of which are visible, were important. But, at the same time, I am sure our ancestors also made use of invisible abilities, which included not only individual intelligence but also teamwork, as humans were rather weak animals in the wild.

In addition, they must have relied on their instincts, most of which we consider ourselves to have already lost. But, maybe those instincts and superhuman abilities are not lost but simply hidden or stored way back in our brain or our DNA. We just do not remember how to tap into those abilities. I think Buddhist or Zen meditation, yoga, religious chanting, deep breathing methods, *qìgōng*, martial arts, etc., are the methods for opening the chakras or discovering the path to enlightenment.

Many readers would agree that Zen meditation, yoga, and *qìgōng* are popular methods for bettering yourself or opening chakras. However, maybe not as many people would agree that training in the martial arts can be a way to achieve enlightenment. This is mostly because we tend to see only the visible part of martial arts such as karate. We focus on how well we can perform *kata* or *kumite*. Unfortunately, not too many people consider the fact that the invisible part is just as—if not more—important.

What is the invisible part of the martial arts? It includes things such as diligence, persistence, honesty, honor, respect, etc. In the average dojo, your sensei may emphasize diligence by asking you to train hard. He may also emphasize respect by having you bow to him and your classmates. He probably encourages you to continue training until you reach a higher rank or a degree of black belt. He is teaching you persistence. Yes, these attributes are very important and must be taught.

On the other hand, do instructors teach much on the importance of being honest, honorable, or free of ego? Yes, they may tell you these things, but are they conducting themselves according to these attributes? Unfortunately, I have witnessed too many instructors buying their *dan* diplomas and falsifying their true ranks. I have also heard that they give examinations to make money. Most instructors, including me, are not perfect. However, we must at least try to minimize our shortcomings.

Some people have told me that they do not mind if an instructor has bad character as long as he is good at his karate skills. I can sort of understand this if it is only a seminar or other temporary teaching scenario. However, many choose to join his dojo, which means they will be around the instructor consistently for possibly many years. This is something I cannot understand. If the instructor is dishonest or full of ego, you will be around this. I have heard of a few instructors who like to beat up their students. Do you want to follow a bully? I really hope not unless you also want to become a bully yourself. If you wish to learn only the techniques of karate, that is called *karatejutsu* (空手術). On the other hand, if you wish to learn the way of karate, called *karatedo* (空手道), that comes as a package of both physical (visible) and mental/spiritual (invisible) sides.

Master Funakoshi believed this. Let me share the five principles contained in the *Dojo Kun* (道場訓) of Shotokan (松濤館). I am sure other styles have their own *Dojo Kun*, and it may be similar to that of Shotokan.

I will show two translations. One is the standard version that is recited by dojo members all around the world. Since this is a recitation, it is intentionally cut short. For that reason, the true or full meaning is hidden. The other is my translation, which I will provide with a more detailed explanation so that the reader can have a better understanding of these *kun*.

OK, here are the five *kun* in Japanese and their translations:

人格完成に努むること
Jinkaku kansei ni tsutomuru koto
Standard recitation: 'Seek perfection of character'
My translation: 'Strive for perfection of character'

In Shotokan, this principle is supposed to be the most important one. Unfortunately, I do not think this is being taught sufficiently.

誠の道を守ること

Makoto no michi o mamoru koto

Standard recitation: 'Be faithful'

My translation: 'Keep the way of truth', 'Always be truthful'

This is also a great principle, but I am afraid it is not being taught in many dojo.

努力の精神を養うこと

Doryoku no seishin o yashinau koto

Standard recitation: 'Endeavor'

My translation: 'Cultivate/develop/grow the spirit of persistence'

礼儀を重んずること

Reigi o omonzuru koto

Standard recitation: 'Respect others'

My translation: 'Develop the spirit of respect [toward the universe]'

This principle of respect expands much further than just to other people. It includes the practitioner himself and everything around him.

血気の勇を戒むること

Kekki no yu o imashimuru koto

Standard recitation: 'Refrain from violent behavior'

My translation: 'Refrain from violent behavior [coming from anger or pride]'

So, what do you think? Do you not think it is interesting that Master Funako-shi did not include any principles at all about the visible physical side? If he had believed the physical side of karate was more important, he would have included something like "Practice *kata* a million times" or "Strengthen your body" or "Practice speeding up your techniques." However, he included none of these ideas. Even though he did teach the physical side of karate, such as *kata* and *kobudo* (古武道), he considered the invisible mental/spiritual side of training to be much more difficult— and thus more important—to attain. I totally agree with him.

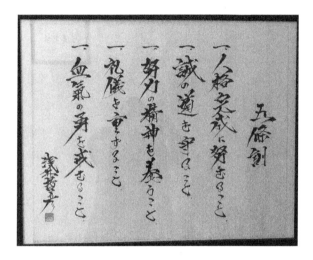

Dojo Kun brushed by Master Tetsuhiko Asai

Master Funakoshi, after retiring from his career as a high school teacher, arrived in mainland Japan at the age of fifty-four without any position or job at all. He taught karate until his death at the age of eighty-nine. His wife stayed on Okinawa to take care of their ancestral grave. He was totally committed to teaching karate to university students in Tokyo, so he never went back to Okinawa. He lived very frugally and never claimed any rank or title. If you learn how he lived and how he taught, I suspect you will respect him and appreciate his philosophy much more.

Some people may argue that if a person's karate skill is great, we do not need to make a big deal about his character. They firmly state that they would go to such an instructor's dojo to learn karate. It is true that they might learn *karate-*

jutsu from him, but he would never be able to teach them true *karatedo*.

Conclusion

As I explained in depth in this chapter, *karatedo* contains both visible and invisible aspects of the way. Once we learn the hardware, we have to expand our ability with regard to the software part of the karate way. In the last chapter of this book, I will reveal and discuss the ultimate goal of karate. I think you will be surprised to find what I consider to be the ultimate goal. You may not agree with my conclusion, but I hope you will evaluate the ideas and concepts that led to my claim. I believe I am the first—and possibly the only—person who has come to the conclusion that you will find in the final chapter. I hope you will be able to study both the visible and the invisible sides of *karatedo*.

CHAPTER FOUR
第四章

OMOTE VS. URA
表と裏の考察

In this chapter, I would like to discuss a very interesting philoso-phy behind two Japanese words: *omote* (表) and *ura* (裏). These two words express completely opposite ideas. *Omote* has many different meanings in Japanese, depending on how and where it is used. In the context of the martial arts, it means 'front', 'surface', or 'exterior'. The other word, *ura*, can mean 'rear', 'back', or 'reverse'. Many *karateka* know *uraken uchi* (裏拳打ち, 'backfist'), so you may be more familiar with the word *ura* than *omote*.

Omote

Ura

I plan to explain the deeper meanings of *omote* and *ura* as these terms go way beyond the meanings of just 'front' and 'back'.

For the simple meanings of 'front' and 'back', we prefer using another set of Japanese terms, which are *mae* and *ushiro*.

For 'front', the kanji 前 is used. This kanji is read as *zen* or *mae*. The reader will be familiar with the karate term *zenkutsu dachi* (前屈立ち), which literally means 'forward-bending stance'. You are probably also familiar with the tech-nique *mae ashi geri* (前足蹴り, 'front leg kick').

For 'back', we use the kanji 後, which is read as *ko* or *ushiro*. You find this kanji in the terms *kokutsu dachi* (後屈立ち, 'backward-bending stance') and *ushiro geri* (後ろ蹴り, 'rear kick').

Since the main subject of this chapter is *omote* and *ura*, I will not go any further into the terms *mae* and *ushiro*. Let us dive more deeply into the meanings of *omote* and *ura* now.

I mentioned earlier that *omote* can mean 'surface' or 'exterior'. These mean-

ings are definitely different from 'front'. This word refers to something that is visible, obvious, or exposed (e.g., the visible side of an object). It also refers to the obverse side of something, such as the side of a coin known as *heads*. *Omote* has another kanji, 面, which can be read as *omote* or *men*. This kanji means 'face' or 'surface' and is used to refer to the front of a structure (e.g., a house, building, store,

etc.) and also a mask (such as the ones used

in *noh* [能]). The equipment used in kendo

(剣道) to protect the face and head is also

called *men*. The equipment used in karate for

a similar purpose is referred to as *menho* or

menpo (面砲 [photo right]).

Omote is the visible side, so it attracts much attention. *Ura*, on the other hand, indicates something that is hidden, invisible, or even secret. Therefore, it does not appear as often, nor is it emphasized as much as *omote*. However, do not let this fool you. What is hidden and invisible can be much more important or valuable. This is the case in the Western world, as well, but it is more so in Japanese culture. Let me give you one example.

A traditional garment for Japanese men is called the *haori* (羽織). It is like a jacket worn over a kimono (着物). If you like samurai movies, I am sure you have seen them. You will also recall that most of them are woven in dark-toned colors such as black, dark blue, or dark brown and that they have no visible designs except for the family crest. But, did you know that many *haori* have

exciting and gorgeous designs inside? The top part of the cloth on the inside of the back of the garment has a bold design that is called *gakuura* (額裏). This particular fashion is for men's *haori* because women's kimono typically display beautiful designs on the visible side. It is known that Japanese men do not show off their fashion.

What do you think of this concept? I wonder if the reader can understand this mentality or if it makes any sense. I suspect it may be rather strange and foreign. This was the true way of thinking for Japanese men, at least in the olden days. They wished to enjoy fashion secretly and to know that these gorgeous designs were visible only on the inside. The tradition seems to have continued as the outside (*omote*) of modern-day *haori* looks conservative with its bland and fairly neutral colors, whereas the inside (*ura*) is still adorned with beautiful and dramatic designs.

OK, there is more to this, and I would like to add one more thought on this particular concept, which is that the popular tendency or general thinking pattern among Japanese people is that what is obvious or visible is not as important or beautiful as what is hidden or invisible. In other words, what is obvious is rather simple and boring. What is hard to find is, in general, better.

Let me give you a few examples. The first is good deeds that go unnoticed. You might have heard that if you lose something in Japan, it is most likely it will be returned. Just imagine if you left a wallet with a lot of cash or your smartphone in a restaurant or at a station. What would happen to the lost item in your city? Most likely you would never see it again. In many cases of returned items in Japan, the finder does not even leave his name, so the person who lost the item does not know who helped him. This is because most Japanese people are proud to do a good thing without any recognition or reward. It is a hidden good deed, which is very popular in Japan. There is a word for this particular behavior: *intoku* 陰徳. This means 'a hidden good deed' or 'secret charity'.

You may remember that the world was impressed by the acts of the Japanese fans at the World Cup in 2018. Many Japanese remained in the stadium after the soccer match was over and started to pick up the trash around them. It happened after most of the games, whether the Japanese team won or lost. Of course, they did not do this out of fear that the stadium would be messy the next day as they knew a professional cleaning team would come in later and clean the place up. You don't know who they were. The only thing you know is that they were Japanese fans who wanted to show their appreciation for the games.

Another example of the mental difference of the Japanese is their tendency to be passive. They do not wish to express their desires or thoughts. If you take a Japanese woman on a date to a restaurant and ask her what she wants to order, she will most likely say, "I will order whatever you pick," or, "Whatever you pick is fine with me."

If you hear this, you will likely think this person does not have her own opinion or a sense of independence. But, what is the explanation here? She definitely has her own opinions and wishes; however, she prefers to keep them hidden (*ura*). To expose things about herself too quickly is not considered to be cultured or wise. She wants to reveal more (*omote*) as she gains your trust. This trend is also seen in Western society; thus, it may not be too difficult to understand. However, the trend you are familiar with is manifested on a much smaller scale, so you might still feel strange.

Interestingly, the Japanese tend to not trust a person who is eloquent. A quiet worker in the office receives much respect instead. I think this is totally opposite of what is found in the Western world, where one must express himself and make his demands in order to move up. If you are too quiet, you will not be considered to be a leader or even to be making a contribution to the team. If you have had the experience of listening to a Japanese karate instructor's explanations, you have probably noticed that they are very short and not very deep. This is not because of his poor English ability; it is just that he prefers not to explain too much.

@Jazzhands16
how do I make a fist?

There are two main reasons for this occurrence. You will have no problem hearing the first; however, I must say it is probably a fifty-fifty situation. Let me explain further.

A learned instructor feels that it is better to give only hints or the general idea rather than explaining the whole subject in detail. This is because he believes students should use these hints to do their own research and investigation in order to learn the full context. Japanese instructors feel that one cannot learn only with words. They believe all students must use their body to back up what they have heard. If you have received a simple reply of "Train more" from your Japanese sensei, he wants you to use your body to experiment and try.

When you ask him, "How can I develop the *seika tanden*?" or, "What is ki?" he feels these things are beyond verbal explanation. If you want to get something tangible, you may want to change your direct questions to something like "Would you give me a hint regarding X, Y, or Z?" If the instructor knows the answer and has a good relationship with you, he will give you something to think about.

The second reason many Japanese instructors do not explain much or just say, "Train more," is simply that they falsely believe Western students will not understand the Japanese mind or Japanese concepts. Believe it or not, it could also be that they do not know the answer. Some Japanese instructors are so proud of themselves that they refuse to admit they don't know something. Even though I am Japanese, I know we are not God, so I am aware that I can be ignorant or incorrect. I have no problem admitting I do not know, but many senior instructors do.

If you wish to maintain a good relationship with a Japanese instructor, it is best not to pursue further or demand an answer when you encounter this situation. I advise you to see if you can change your direct question to an indirect one. If you can get some kind of a hint, then just continue your training as you think about it. After training for a year or so, see if you still have the same question. You may be surprised as you may discover the answer on your own.

Yes, these examples are about the mind and culture of the Japanese, but how about their body? As this is not the main subject of this chapter, I will share only one example of how the Japanese value the unseen part (*ura*) more than what is

exposed (*omote*). An excellent example is the appearance of the body, that is, how a person looks.

In the Western world, I find weightlifting to be very popular among men. They proudly show off their well-defined chest muscles and biceps. They seem to epitomize the concept of being manly or desirable. In Japan, on the other hand, though we receive much influence from the Western world, we do not have this inclination.

In the previous chapter, I introduced you to a world beyond what we can see with our eyes. A similar thing can be said about women. A girl with large breasts or hips is considered to be sexy in the Western world. On the other hand, a Japanese girl who is "gifted" with such physical characteristics would consider them to be embarrassing and would view them as a problem to be dealt with. She would wear baggy clothes to hide her figure.

Does this mean the Japanese do not care about the attractiveness of the body? No, it does not mean that. In fact, they care a lot about how they look, but it is certainly expressed in a different way. Japanese women prefer tall guys to short ones. At the same time, they look for other qualities that are not so obvious, such as honesty, sincerity, dependability, etc. A rich guy with a fancy sports car is not necessarily a popular guy in Japan. Similarly, in Japan, a skinny girl can be very popular if she brightens her face with an attractive smile and acts with feminine manners.

I think we have covered this area more than enough. We should get back to the concept of *omote* and *ura* in the context of the martial arts. Now you can see that *omote* and *ura* do not simply refer to the positions of front and back.

Did you know that the word *urawaza* (裏技) is used frequently in judo (柔道), aikido (合気道), and kendo? It is not used too often in karate, so you might not have heard it. However, by now, you know that *ura* refers to something that is hidden or secret. Also, *waza* (技) is a popular word for 'technique'. Thus, you can guess the meaning of this term. It is understood to be an unorthodox technique, underhanded technique, or hidden/secret technique.

I have already mentioned that the word *ura* is found in some common karate terms, such as *uraken uchi*, and *ura mawashi geri* (裏回し蹴り, 'reverse

roundhouse kick' [photo right]). One of the
kata-training methods employed at ASAI is
mirror-image *kata* called *ura no kata* (裏の
形) or *gyaku no kata* (逆の形). The word
gyaku is also used in *gyaku zuki* (逆突き,
'reverse punch'), so *gyaku* means 'reverse'.

Just in case you are not familiar with
ura or *gyaku no kata*, I will explain briefly how it is done. As you know, all of the
Heian (平安) *kata* start to the left, that is, toward the nine-o'clock position. To
practice *ura no kata*, you start to the right, that is, toward the three-o'clock position. In the case of Tekki (鉄騎), the first step is always to the right side. So, with
ura no kata, you start Tekki to the left side. This is an excellent training method
for breaking routines and mindsets. It was practiced frequently in the past, but,
unfortunately, it does not seem to have been adopted by many instructors lately.

In karate, we do not use the word
omote too often. In fact, I have never
heard it used in my sixty years of dojo
life. However, in other martial arts, such
as kenjutsu, aikido, and judo, the term
omote waza (表技) is used to describe
standard or regular techniques (as opposed to *ura waza*, which are counters or
hidden techniques).

OK, you may say, "I understand the meaning of *omote* and *ura*, but we rarely
use these terms in karate. So, why are you talking about them?" An excellent
question. In fact, this question leads me to a very fascinating and unique concept
that we find not only in karate but also in all martial arts in general. I guarantee
that you will understand karate better and appreciate it more by simply knowing
this concept.

The concept that is shared among the arts in Japan, including the martial arts,
is their multilayered structure and training process. Before I explain this con-

cept further, I would like to bring up some comparative concepts in the Western world.

As an example, I will use a full-contact fighting sport called *boxing*, where they specialize in punching. I am not going to explain the differences found in the techniques but rather in the training method. I have never received formal training in boxing, so if my description is incorrect, I will have to apologize. Also, I am simply pointing out the differences and definitely not trying to criticize nor belittle boxing.

When you join a boxing club, you learn different punching methods such as the jab, hook, uppercut, straight punch, etc. Then, you learn how to block, sway, duck, etc., as well as the footwork necessary for getting in and getting out. Another thing you have to do is build up your body to toughen up your midsection so that you can endure receiving punches. You also need to do a lot of skipping rope to sharpen your footwork and jog for many miles to build up your endurance.

You then start hitting punching bags, and pretty soon you have a sparring partner to practice free sparring with. Initially, the sparring partner may act as only a receiver so that you will not be too scared or intimidated as a beginner. Some boxing gyms may have a more defined training menu, but I suspect that the general idea of training is as described above. Boxers get better as they build their body and accumulate many hours of experience in free sparring.

In a traditional dojo in Japan, a white belt would never get involved in *jiyu kumite* (自由組手, 'free sparring'). This tradition used to be followed in overseas dojo, but, due to the popularity of tournaments, I have seen many dojo allow, or even encourage, their white belts to engage in *jiyu kumite*. I am afraid this is an unfortunate trend in sport or tournament karate.

Anyway, in karate, we have a defined training program, which includes *kihon*, *kata*, and *kumite*. We also do exercises, but our main training components are those three *K*s. Again, I am not saying this system is better than that of boxing. I am simply saying that traditional karate has a clearly defined program and that it is layered.

In other words, the *kihon* and *kata* requirements become more complex and challenging as the student advances in rank. By the way, boxing does not have the *kata* training system.

Even the *kumite* structure is layered. For beginners, we have *gohon kumite* (五本組手, 'five-attack sparring'). As you advance, you move up to *sanbon kumite* (三本組手, 'three-attack sparring') and then to *ippon kumite* (一本組手, 'single-attack sparring'). Even when you become a brown belt by spending more than a year diligently training, you still do *jiyu ippon* kumite (自由一本組手, 'semifree sparring'). You are not allowed to engage in full free sparring until you reach first-degree black belt.

Again, I am simply explaining the concept of the training system in most traditional karate dojo. I am sure the finer points of training may differ, but that does not matter. Interestingly, some people (mostly parents) criticize this system, saying that it is for commercial purposes. In other words, they say this complex system is structured this way for the purpose of making money.

In this system, students must take an exam to advance in rank, say, every three months or so. By creating this structure, the instructor can award colored belts to his students. Each belt comes with a different exam syllabus. The dojo charges the students for the exam as well as the diploma and the new belt, which are commercial objec- tives. I am aware that some dojo do this for this reason, but I also know that many others do it because they believe the layered structure is good for the students.

OK, though I strongly believe that a layered learning structure is better than natural development, I will not go into that here. The main aim of this chapter is to understand the hidden aspects of the layers themselves. This subject gets deeper and more interesting as we dig further into this concept.

So, let's take the belt system. What is visible (*omote*) here is obviously a group of colors starting with white and ending with black. Each student climbs up the ladder by taking an exam every three to six months, depending on the policy of the dojo.

But, there is also a hidden meaning (*ura*) to this that has both a positive and a possibly negative perspective. The positive side is the motivation for students to practice so that they can get promoted. The negative side is that a dishonorable instructor could use this system only to make money.

Once a student attains a black belt, there are no more different colors. What happens then is a change in the promotion structure. The student is given a rank, such as first-, second-, third-degree black belt, etc., but others cannot see his

rank just by looking at his plain black belt (*omote*). In some styles, stripes are applied to the belts to show rank (image left). In judo, Brazilian jujutsu, and some Oki-nawan styles, they award red belts to indicate the ranks of ninth- and tenth-degree black belt. This is only my personal opinion, but I dislike this idea as I think it is vain and shows a lack of humility.

I shared the above examples just to show some simple cases of *omote* and *ura*. However, these are not the really interesting part of this concept. What is important is what is found in the training and techniques.

For example, when we teach *soto uke* (外受け, outside block') to you as a white belt, we tell you to bring your arm way behind your head and move it in a large circular motion toward the front.

We may add that there should be a wrist twist at the end of the motion. Regardless, the key emphasis is on large motion. This is true with all other techniques. This is *omote*, and, in this case, it does not mean 'visible' but rather more like 'standard'. In other words, it is what a correct technique should look like.

So, that motion is proper for a white belt. However, as you advance to the higher ranks, such as first-degree black belt, your technique will look somewhat different. Invariably, your technique will look smaller. Some people may call it cheating or even say it's incorrect. However, this is most likely not the case.

That smaller technique is correct for a *karateka* of that level. How could there be two different but correct ways to execute the same technique? Let me give you a familiar example that you have experienced in school. When you learned how to write the alphabet for the first time in your life, I am  sure your teacher taught you to make an *A* in the print style. Eventually, however, you learned how to write it in cursive. Both letters are correct, though they look different.

In other words, your technique must change (that is, improve) as your skill level advances. This is the very important part that many practitioners misunderstand. Many falsely believe they need to stick to the original teaching and that to change is to cheat or to be mistaken. In other words, as you become more experienced and proficient, you need to move your body more efficiently. This does not always mean your movements will be smaller. The movements could be larger or even the same, but they should be more efficient.

 How could it be more efficient if the movements are the same? To make it more visible and easier for the reader to imagine, let's think of *seiken zuki* (正拳, 'standard-fist punch'). A punch executed by a white belt is slower and less powerful. The same punch thrown by a black belt is visibly faster and stronger. It is not because this black belt is bigger or younger. Even if

these two practitioners have an identical build and are of the same age, you know there will be a difference in performance.

Why? Well, you know the reason. The black belt has learned how to relax certain muscles and tense only the necessary ones. The white belt, on the other hand, will most likely tense all of his arm and shoulder muscles, believing that is the correct way to generate speed and power. Of course, this futile effort has the opposite effect on his performance. In addition, he may not know when to inhale, exhale, or hold his breath. Learning the things that may be invisible is a technique in and of itself.

Now I need to discuss another important but rare subject, which is the importance of vision in our daily life, and thus also in karate training. I am sure the reader will agree with this. When you engage in *kumite* training, your teacher tells you to look at the opponent intensely and carefully. This makes sense. Here you must pay attention not only to his minute movements (*omote*) but also to his intention (*ura*), which is more important. Unless you can read and understand both sides, you may not be able to react correctly to his attacks.

Your instructor may tell you to do the same in *kata*, which you perform without a visible opponent. I understand that some people were taught to practice *kumite* like *kata* and vice versa. Though I do not fully agree, in a way, I understand the purpose of this teaching. Regardless, it is difficult to realize this when you are inexperienced. It becomes easier as you train for many years. This is a good example of layered training.

TWO SIDES
OF THE SAME COIN

In conclusion, I hope the reader understands that, in karate training, what is invisible (*ura*) is just as important as what is visible (*omote*), if not more so. They are like two sides of the same coin. Do you not agree that we need both sides, regardless of which side may be more or less important?

CHAPTER FIVE
第五章

WHY IS DEATH IMPORTANT?
死は何故重要か

To consider death, we need to go back in history to the time of the samurai. To them, *bushido* (武士道) was critical. So, what is *bushido*? There is a well-known quote regarding this question by a samurai from Saga Prefecture (佐賀県) named Tsunetomo Yamamoto (山本常朝, 1659–1719). In his book, *Hagakure* (葉隠, '*Hidden Leaves*'), which is also called *The Book of the Samurai* and was com-

piled from 1709 to 1716, he makes the following famous statement: "*Bushido to wa shinu koto to mitsuketari* (武士道とは死ぬことと見つけたり)." The literal meaning is 'I have found that *bushido*

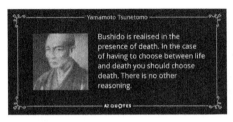

means to die'. In other words, according to him, a samurai must live as though he were already dead or could kill himself at that very moment.

This concept is very understandable as samurai were soldiers. There were constant wars and battles between the samurai clans during the Sengoku (戦国, 'Warring States') period of the fifteenth and sixteenth centuries. During that period, all samurai were at risk of dying at any moment. In fact, thousands died in battle. During this period, no one needed to ask what *bushido* was. They were all willing to die bravely. Their dream was to die honorably in an important battle.

However, one samurai lord, Ieyasu Tokugawa (徳川家康, 1543–1616) started to rule Japan as the first shogun of the Tokugawa shogunate, or Edo shogunate, in the early seventeenth century. His domain and system were stable and lasted more than two hundred fifty years, a time that is referred to as the *Edo period*. Even though there were a few skirmishes among some of the remote samurai clans, basically, all of Japan enjoyed a peaceful time without war during the Edo period, which was quite unique for that period in the perspective of world history. This lasted until the early nineteenth century, when emissaries of Western countries such as the U.S., the UK, and Russia came and demanded the opening of the ports.

As a consequence of this extended peacetime, the samurai were no longer called to action. In addition, the shogunate enacted the policy of *kenka ryo seibai*

(喧嘩両成敗), which dictated that in the event of a quarrel, both parties would be punished by death, regardless of reason or fault. It is incredible that if a samurai drew his sword for any reason whatsoever, including self-defense, he would have received a sentence of capital punishment by *seppuku* (切腹), or *harakiri* (腹切).

Due to this policy and the lack of battles, life-or-death situations totally disappeared for hundreds of years. Can you imagine the psychological consequences for the samurai? Probably very easily. Sadly, they became mentally lax. Initially, they kept their samurai spirit, but, after a hundred years of total peace, many of them eventually forgot this spirit or even became somewhat cowardly. Some of the more serious samurai were concerned.

It was during this time, in the early eighteenth century, that *Hagakure* came out. In other words, Yamamoto had to remind the samurai that they must not forget that they need to face the concept of death if they wished to call themselves samurai. A hundred years of peace was spoiling the spirit of the samurai, and Yamamoto had to sound the alarm.

THE HAGAKURE

Yamamoto Tsunetomo

葉
隠

太出
馬健

The Heart of the Warrior

D. E. Tarver
The Warrior Series Book Three

OK, this was for the samurai, and they were the soldiers. But, why am I bringing up this subject here? Is there any kind of relationship to us as *karateka*? My quick answer is yes, there is. In fact, I must emphasize that there is a strong relationship. Sadly, most of us are not aware of this as the current trend of karate is leaning heavily toward sport karate. Even if some *karateka* happen to be aware of the importance, most do not consider it to be too relevant to their daily lives.

I decided to write this chapter because I have the same critical concern that Yamamoto, the author of *Hagakure*, felt some three hundred years ago. There are several key reasons I consider this subject to be extremely important. In this chapter, I would like to share the two most serious reasons.

The first reason is that the samurai lived in a peaceful time just as we do. Thus, they ignored or avoided the idea of death, and we are doing exactly the same thing.

Yamamoto reminded the samurai of that period what the true samurai spirit was. It was to face death willingly. In other words, this peaceful time had lasted many years, and the samurai were forgetting this important concept of ultimate bravery, which was the core principle of the samurai. Life during the period in which he lived was "too peaceful"; therefore, he felt the samurai were spoiled and had become cowardly and thus needed to make a conscious effort to think about death.

Most readers are most likely living in a peaceful society similar to that of Yamamoto. Naturally, his time was the samurai age of some three hundred years ago. But, the ultimate bravery of sacrificing one's life is not required of most citizens of the twenty-first century. If that is true, then why am I writing about this subject?

I am aware that this is a very heavy and controversial subject indeed as few like to talk about death or dying. And yet, I feel I must cover this subject in this

book because I firmly believe this is the essence of not only *bushido* but also *karatedo*. Sadly, it is true that the subject of death and dying is very much disliked and also feared. Thus, this subject is conveniently ignored and often avoided.

Many readers may not like this important subject, and if you wish to ignore it, of course, it is your choice to skip this chapter. However, I consider this chapter to be one of the most important ones in this book, and I hope the reader will buckle down and take this journey with me.

We all know that thousands of people are dying every day, but you normally do not see this happen unless you work in a hospital or as a policeman. Moreover, we all know that one day it will happen to everyone, including you and me. But, interestingly to me, we try not to think about it. We almost believe that we will live forever. When a baby is born, we have a big party and tell everyone. We all love to attend a party for a newborn baby, and this makes us very happy.

On the other hand, a funeral is not openly publicized and, naturally, is not celebrated. Sometimes we may keep this very confidential and very quiet. You may consider this phenomenon to be so natural that you do not think twice about it. In our society, we can say that these are our social mores. Some people may consider me strange, but I find it very interesting that a newborn baby arrives in the world crying and unhappy, whereas a dead person, on the other hand, is very quiet and has a peaceful look. I feel that a baby is not happy to leave the spirit world, while a dead person is happy to return there. Am I crazy to think this? Have you thought about this?

The second reason is that the concept of facing and peacefully accepting death was the standard for the samurai.

This second reason is more important. I believe that the concept of facing and accepting death is the ultimate goal of modern-day martial arts. Many readers may think that the above statement is an exaggeration or even incorrect. Despite this, I truly believe this is the most important objective if karate is practiced as *budo*. Let me explain why I believe this to be true.

First of all, we must agree that *budo* is said to be the art of killing. In karate training, we learn how to punch and kick our opponent. We are taught that our punches should be executed according to the concept of *ikken hissatsu* (一拳必殺, 'one punch, certain kill'). Many of us regularly punch a *makiwara* (巻藁) to toughen up our knuckles. In other words, we are making our fists our weapons. We are supposed to "kill" our enemies when we fight. Of course, we are not en-

couraged to engage in real fights, but we certainly practice karate for the purposes of self-defense. In fact, self-defense is the most popular reason people give when they are asked why they started karate practice. So, you want to have

the ability to kill when you have to protect yourself from an intruder, an armed robber, or even a bully.

Yes, we all understand this when we are talking about the death of the enemy. However, I stated above that the concept of facing and accepting death was the goal of *karatedo*. In other words, I was referring to our own death. Yes, the tables are now turned, and this makes a big difference, doesn't it? You may ask, "Why do we have to accept death? We want to avoid death, not accept it." This is an excellent point that touches on the core of the samurai spirit.

At the beginning of this chapter, I quoted the key statement from Yamamoto's book, *Hagakure*. I translated it and then said the meaning of that statement was that a samurai must live as though he were already dead or could kill himself at that very moment. OK, that was for the samurai, and you can understand it. However, many readers may think this is not relevant to them as *karateka*. This is exactly why I am writing this chapter. I differ from those who would consider this idea to be irrelevant.

This difference in our beliefs stems from the difference in our concept of self-defense. Most people consider self-defense to be the ability to fight off a bully, a drunk guy at a bar, a guy with a case of road rage, or someone like that. Believe me, if you are practicing karate for the sole purpose of fighting off one of these kinds of people, you are wasting your time. The structured training of traditional karate for most practitioners at the level of *shodan* would not help too much in a street fight. An experienced street fighter could easily take you out. If street fighting is what you want, you should go to a boxing gym or practice MMA.

Some may say, "No, I am not thinking about defending myself against these people. I am thinking about a more serious situation. I want to defend myself against a thief who wants to take my wallet." This sounds like real self-defense. However, I do not think karate should be practiced for this purpose. The thief may have a gun or a knife. Why would you risk your life for a wallet? If a thief wants to steal your car, let him have the car. Do you consider your car to be more valuable than your life? Of course not. We must not blame a victim or consider him to be a coward if he complies with a thief and lets him have his wallet or car. Instead of using karate to fight off a car thief, avoid these unfortunate situations by using wise judgment and common sense, such as not driving through unsafe areas or parking in unlit areas at night.

Then, what kind of situation am I practicing karate for? I am practicing only for situations in which I have to defend not only my own life but also that of my friends or family. I can think of two situations right now.

The first situation would be the hijacking of a plane. If I happened to be on a hijacked plane, and the hijacker were trying to crash the plane into a building, I know exactly what I would do. Even if I knew the guy would try to kill me, I would stand up and try to stop him. Even if I got killed, I would consider my life to have been well spent if that action could save the other passengers. Even if I failed and the plane crashed, the outcome would still be the same. I would have used my samurai spirit and tried my best, though the odds were totally against me. Standing up would be what mattered.

Another sure situation would be if an intruder broke into my house. I consider my house to be my castle, and I am responsible for protecting everyone within my house. If someone broke into my house at night and I were there, I would fight until he killed me or I killed or subdued him. During the struggle, my family members would call the police. If the intruder shot me, that would make a huge noise, and he would most likely run away. This means that, even if I got killed, my family members would remain safe. Then, I would consider my life to have been well spent.

So, both of the situations I brought up have a high risk of loss of life. When you think about it, something like this would happen maybe less than once in a lifetime. But, that is exactly what you should be training for. You need to train more in the mental than in the physical aspects of self-defense.

As I mentioned in Chapter 3: "The Mystery of the Visible and the Invisible," Master Funakoshi left us a valuable teaching in the fifth principle of his *Niju Kun*, in which he states that mental technique is more important than physical technique. Many people misunderstand this to be referring to the development of a fighting spirit. However, I believe he was referring to having the ultimate courage to give up your life. I believe he was telling us that no matter how hard we practice our karate techniques, if we are not ready to die for a cause, we did not learn the true spirit of karate.

Conclusion

If you are seeking true *budo* karate, or if you refer to your karate as *budo*, *bujutsu*, or *martial art*, you must go beyond the common belief that your karate is good enough if you can take out a bully or a drunk guy at a bar. We must never forget that the martial arts are a set of skills that are designed for killing a person.

Therefore, we must choose very carefully when to use this skill set. If a guy bumps into you, simply apologize, even if it was not your fault. If a guy wants to cut in front of your car, let him. Do not accept a silly challenge as it is not important enough to waste your time and energy on. If a thief with a handgun or a knife wants your wallet, your smartphone, or even your car, give it to him. Believe me, your life, as well as that of your companions, is much more valuable than cash, credit cards, or any other material thing. Do not be a dead hero.

This skill set must be reserved only for life-or-death situations. This could involve a hijacker, an intruder, or even a mass shooter. You should risk your life to protect the lives of your friends, your family, or even your next-door neighbors. When it involves a criminal with a gun, you need to fight with the intent to kill him before he kills you. Can you do this? You need to prepare for it mentally more than physically.

Therefore, when you practice karate, you must always train your mind to accept death in a critical situation. You must be mentally prepared to lose your life. If you do not have this mindset at that critical moment, you may act cowardly or freeze and do nothing. This dishonor is something every *budo karateka* wants to avoid as it is often worse than death.

CHAPTER SIX
第六章

WHEN DOES DEATH OCCUR?
死亡は何時起こるか

This may be considered to be an easy question, but is it really? In fact, the answer can be very blurry and unclear. First of all, there are two different sets of criteria. One is for legal death, and the other is for clinical death.

According to USLegal,

legal death refers to a situation where a person is considered dead under law. A person is usually considered legally dead after a legal pronouncement by a qualified person that further medical care is not appropriate. The specific criteria used to pronounce legal death are variable and often depend on the circumstances in order to pronounce a person legally dead. Brain death is an example of a scenario in which legal death is pronounced. In the U.S., brain death is legal in every state except the states of New York and New Jersey, where the law requires that a person's lungs and heart must also have stopped before it can be declared that a person is legally dead. (definitions.uslegal.com/l/legal-death/)

For a long time, we used to believe that a person's death was determine by the fact that the heart had stopped. However, with the advancement of modern medicine, the line between life and death has become blurred.

The article "Clinically Dead? The Blurred Line between Life and Death" by Tia Ghose explains the definition of clinical or biological death. Here is an excerpt:

Despite its frequent use, the term "clinical death" doesn't actually have a consistent meaning, said Dr. James Bernat, a neurologist at Dartmouth College's Geisel School of Medicine in New Hampshire. In most hospitals, the doctor in charge of a patient's care makes the death determination, and there aren't universal guidelines for when to make that call, he said.

"You're dead when a doctor says you're dead," Bernat told Live Science.

Until the 1950s, death was considered to be the point when any one of the vital functions—heartbeat, electrical brain activity or respiration—ceased. Once one part of the system failed, then the others would soon shut down as well, the reasoning went.

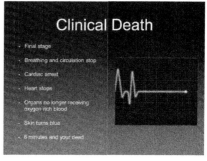

But the advent of the mechanical ventilator, which pushes air into and out of the lungs, created a new category called brain death, Bernat said.

That led to a whole class of people with warm bodies and circulating blood—who could even fight off infections or gestate a baby—but who had absolutely no brain function, said Leslie Whetstine, a philosopher at Walsh University in Ohio who studies the definitions of death.

To be declared brain-dead, a person must have irreversibly lost function in all parts of his or her brain. Doctors make that call by performing neurological exams to search for electrical brain activity, or blood circulation to the brain, as well as a test to see if the patient attempts to breathe when the ventilator is turned off. (www.livescience.com/46418-clinical-death-definitions.html)

OK, you may say, "Thank you for the explanation of death. But, I do not understand why you are discussing this in a book about karate. What has this got to do with karate or the martial arts?" An excellent question. I wrote this chapter to present the idea that there is another definition of the death of a person.

I believe a person is not dead just because a doctor or a legal person defines him as dead. Yes, you may have a funeral, and the body may be buried or cremated. Despite this, a person continues to "live" as long as someone remembers him. My parents have physically passed away, but they live, at least in me. There are other relatives who remember my parents, as well. So, my parents live in their memory.

Do you not agree? If you have someone who was dear to you but passed, does he not live as long as you remember him? I truly believe this. If a person is forgotten by all, and no one remembers

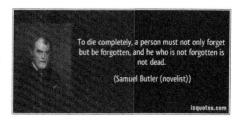

him, then that person is indeed dead for
the last time.

Some famous people agree with me.
Samuel Butler (1835–1902), an English
novelist, said, "To die completely, a
person must not only forget but be forgotten, and he who is not forgotten is not
dead." Again, Tess Gerritsen (1953–), an American novelist and retired physician,
said, "Only the forgotten are truly dead."

This was the very reason I created my organization, ASAI, to remember my karate master, Tetsuhiko
Asai (浅井哲彦, 1935–2006). Everyone who knew
him agrees that Master Asai was a karate genius and
was one of the greatest Shotokan masters of all time.
There are many videos of his actions, and he was
featured in many books and magazines.

Master Asai passed away in 2006, sixteen years ago. Many young practitioners, including some black belts, have never seen or heard of him, let alone met
him. He created many advanced *kata*. If these *kata* are not practiced, they will
be forgotten. He was known for many unique and devastating techniques, such
as *tenshin* (転身, 'body rotation'), whipping-arm or whipping-leg techniques,
short-distance fighting methods, etc. If these are not practiced, they will also be
forgotten.

Shotokan is a long-distance fighting method that incorporates long stances
and long-range techniques. Master Asai supplemented Shotokan with the short-
distance fighting techniques he had learned from White Crane kung fu during his
stay on Taiwan. This bold change was dramatic. Many of his karate colleagues
did not appreciate it because they could not easily master the new techniques. He
had to leave his home organization, the Japan Karate Association (日本空手協会
[JKA]), to start over on his own. He was able to teach his style only after he had
become independent.

You can feel and appreciate his contribution to karate only when you learn Asai *kata* and Asai techniques. What you learn is different from what you would learn in the training found in a standard Shotokan dojo. Many of the techniques are challenging but, at the same time, exciting.

I am sure Master Asai would have wanted to see his *kata* and techniques remembered despite the fact that he might not have expected his name to be remembered. By using his name as the name of my organization, I hope to cause both his techniques and his name to be remembered for many years. I felt it was my responsibility to keep him alive by naming my organization after him.

Chapter Seven
第七章

What Is the Most Lethal Karate Style?
最強の空手流派とは？

There are many styles of karate. They say
there are sixteen main styles and many
more lesser-known styles. We will discuss this more later in this chapter. Styles
are called *ryuha* (流派) in Japanese. The

character for *ryu* means 'flow' or 'style', and the character for *ha* means 'faction'
or 'school'.

Which karate style do you think is the best or most lethal? This is a subject
many people spend much time discussing or arguing about. Many practitioners
believe the style they practice is the best, and they spend a lot of energy explaining and trying to prove why they believe so.

If you have been practicing, say, Shotokan for twenty or thirty years, you
will believe it is the best style. This belief is probably the same if you are a Goju
Ryu, Shito Ryu (糸東流), or Shorin Ryu (少林流) practitioner. Now, these are
all traditional styles that are also called *noncontact styles*. Some people believe
that contact karate is closer to "real" karate. So, if you happen to be a full-contact
karate student, such as a Kyokushinkai (極真会) practitioner, you may believe

you practice the best karate style.

I am not here to compare the merits or advan-
tages of the different styles because I do not believe
there is a best karate style, regardless of whether it is
a contact or noncontact style. Frankly, comparisons
and arguments among the styles is nonsense and a
waste of time.

Let's look at another example. Rugby, soccer, and American football are all
considered to be kinds of football. You may have a preference as to which one
you like to watch or play, but do you not agree that it is nonsense to argue which
is the best football?

On the other hand, we must ask and study why we have so many different
styles that are categorized as methods of hand-to-hand combat. I think this is a

good question. There may be more than a dozen noncontact styles and perhaps half a dozen different contact styles. In addition, there are some fully armored styles, which are only Japanese or Okinawan styles. If you include fighting styles from Korea, China, Russia, the Philippines, India, etc., then the number increases to well over a hundred. Nobody knows the exact figure, but, according to the article "Kung Fu History and Style Guide" by Robert Rousseau, Chinese kung fu alone has more than four hundred substyles (www.liveabout.com/history-and-style-guide-kung-fu-2308273).

The different styles appeared due to different situations, environments, cultural and social conditions, and requirements. In addition, despite having the same human body parts, we have so many different physical characteristics. Some people are muscular, but many are not. Some people are short, while others are tall. If these differ-  ent types of people start a karate style, I am sure their styles will be different. In fact, the kung fu styles that were invented in northern China, where it is very mountainous, have many jumps, kicks, and high stances. Meanwhile, the kung fu styles that were formulated in southern China, where the land is rather flat, have less jumping and kicking and use lower stances.

OK, we understand that there are many different karate styles. And, I claimed earlier that there was no best style. So, I guess you will ask, "How should I pick a style that is best suited for me?" This is also an excellent question, but, at the same time, it can be a very difficult question.

If you are a person who wishes to start karate training, most likely you have no idea that there are many different karate styles. A certain style may be best suited for a muscular person, while another style may mesh well with a smaller, lighter person. There may also be another kind of problem for you if you want to find an excellent style. Even if you know about and select a style, what happens if there is no dojo that teaches that style? Again, even if you find a dojo that teaches that style, what happens if the instructor is not qualified or has very poor teaching skills?

My answer to this question is very simple and straightforward. I believe whichever style you choose is the best style for you. I sincerely believe this statement and am not making it irresponsibly. Let me explain why I stand on this belief.

First of all, let me share how I got into my karate life. I will not go into any detail, but it is necessary to explain to you how I came across Shotokan and how it was destined to be my style. When I was ten years old, I started my martial-arts journey with judo. By training in judo, I found out about karate and wanted to switch to that. I looked for a dojo and, by chance, discovered a Shotokan dojo in my hometown of Kobe. It was purely by accident that I saw an advertisement for this dojo at a train station one day. I was fifteen years old when my karate journey started. Therefore, I have been practicing the same art for sixty years as I am now seventy-five years old as of this year.

During my karate journey, I have practiced Goju Ryu and Kyokushinkai for one year each in order to expand my karate experience. Goju Ryu was—and maybe still is—a very popular karate style in my region, Kansai (関西), that was founded by Chojun Miyagi (宮城長順,

1888–1953) nearly a hundred years ago. Kyokushinkai is well known as a full-

contact karate style that was founded by a famous *karateka*, Masutatsu Oyama (大山倍達, 1923–1994). I learned these fighting methods, and what I learned was and still is beneficial to my understanding of *budo* karate. But, even though I found their methods to be very effective—in some cases even more so than Shotokan—I still loved my style and stayed with it.

I even lived in Tokyo for nearly three years (1997–2000) and attended the famous Nishino Dojo in Shibuya in order to learn how to control opponents with ki without touching them. The exercises were very interesting and helped my flexibility, but the "great" master could not show me or teach me the techniques that I wanted so much to learn. I wrote about my experience at Nishino Dojo in detail in Chapter 13: "Tenketsu Jutsu" of my book *Shotokan Mysteries*, so I will not bore you with the story here. Regardless, I continued to search for the best karate for me.

Luckily, I discovered Asai Ryu (浅井流) in 2001, which was founded by Master Tetsuhiko Asai. This style is a combination of the hard, long-distance fighting method of standard Shotokan karate and the soft, short-distance fighting method of White Crane kung fu, which is known as *hakutsuru ken* (白鶴拳 [read as *báihèchuán* in Chinese]). These two styles complement each other almost seamlessly and merged well to become the new style called *Asai Ryu*. I have been training in this style for the last eighteen years or so, and I could not be happier with what I practice. I personally consider it to be the best style, at least for me.

So, if I had not found a Shotokan dojo when I was a junior high school student, I would not have discovered my best style in the end. Was it an accident that I came across that advertisement at the station? Maybe it was. But, maybe it was not. In Japan, we have a god of martial arts. We believe if you search seriously for a martial art or instructor, this god will arrange the encounter. So, whether you believe this folklore or not, I believe I was meant to find Shotokan.

Now, I want to make sure to emphasize that this chapter is not intended to promote Shotokan or Asai Ryu karate. I just wanted to share an example in order to tell you that whatever style you may choose is the right one. But, there are two conditions to my statement. One is that you must be looking for *budo*. The other is that you have to love it and continue your martial-arts journey for the rest of your life. It will certainly require more than fifty years, although it may be somewhat fewer years for some more talented people. If you are impatient, it will definitely not happen. If you prove to be consistent and dedicated, on the other hand, the god of martial arts will crown you with the best karate style.

Conclusion

Despite the fact that there is no best karate style for everyone, the best karate style for you is the very style you are practicing. After many years of training, your body will be molded to fit the style, and it will become the best karate style for your body. Therefore, my recommendation to those who are searching for "the best karate style" is to seek out the best one you can find now and start practicing.

If the style, dojo, or instructor you picked first does not work out for whatever reason, do not give up. Continue to search for new opportunities. It may take a little time, but you will find your ultimate home eventually. You may be lucky and find your home from the very beginning, but for most people, the journey will have some bumps and even dead ends. Ninety-nine percent of the people who start karate training will drop out before they find the best karate style for them. The difference between those who leave and those who remain is not talent or style. It is that they did not give up and continued training. After forty or fifty years of training, you will find the best karate style for you. Once you find it, how could you give it up?

CHAPTER EIGHT
第八章

THERE CAN BE MYSTERY IN VICTORY, BUT THERE IS NO MYSTERY IN DEFEAT
勝ちに不思議の勝ちあり、負けに不思議の負けなし

The saying *Kachi ni fushigi no kachi ari, make ni fushigi no make nashi* (勝ちに不思議の勝ちあり、負けに不思議の負けなし) is quite famous in Japan. It was created by a samurai named Kiyoshi Matsuura (松浦清, 1760–1841 [image below]). Before I explain what this famous saying is all about, I would like to introduce Matsuura as he was truly an interesting samurai.

First of all, he was not a regular samurai. In fact, he was one of the regional lords of the Hirado Domain (平戸藩), which is in present-day Nagasaki Prefecture (長崎県). He was the oldest son of the eighth lord of Hirado, Masanobu Matsuura (松浦政信, 1735–1771), who died when Seizan was twelve years old. At the age of sixteen, he inherited the domain and became the ninth lord of Hirado.

If that were the only thing that made him unique, I would not have paid this much attention to him. What makes him truly interesting is that he was a person who embodied the concept of *bunburyodo* (文武両道), which means he excelled in both literary and martial arts. In 1806, he retired from his position of lord of Hirado, and, in 1821, he started to write a collection of essays entitled *Kasshi Yawa* (甲子夜話). He continued writing the essays for twenty years until his death. The collection comes in three volumes, which consist of 100, 100, and 78 chapters, respectively.

Since he was young, he learned different martial arts and excelled in many of them. For instance, he received *menkyo kaiden* (免許皆伝, 'license of mastery') in the swordsmanship styles of Shinkage Ryu (新陰流), Tamiya Ryu (田宮流), and, at the age of fifty-three, Shingyoto Ryu (心形刀流). He also received *menkyo kaiden* in the archery style of Heki Ryu (日置流) at the age of sixty-eight. In addition, he trained in Sekiguchi Ryu (関口流), which is a style of jujutsu (柔

術), Shinto Ryu (新当流) horsemanship, Buei Ryu (武衛流) artillery, and a style of sojutsu (槍術), which is a spear art.

His accomplishments in the samurai martial arts are quite impressive. If he had lived in the Sengoku period of the fifteenth and sixteenth centuries, such mastery of various arts would not have been rare or unique. However, Matsuura was born in the eighteenth century, and his training continued well into the nineteenth century, which was the latter part of the peaceful Edo period that I mentioned before.

In the early part of the Edo period, most samurai trained in and mastered the martial arts, and that was expected. However, during the second half of that period, it was quite different, especially toward the end, when Matsuura was training. Some samurai did not practice kenjutsu at all and carried lightweight fake swords. Many of them also sold off their family armor, known as *kacchu* (甲胄), and even their swords.

Since he is such an interesting and unique person, I would like to share more about him. According to the information I found, Matsuura had an excellent memory since childhood. However, he was sickly when he was a child, and his family feared that he might not be able to live to adulthood. In order to improve his health, his grandmother, who was in charge of his education, sent him to a kenjutsu and jujutsu dojo. This proved to be the right remedy. After becoming the head of Hirado, he established a local school, Ishinkan (維新館, 'Hall of Restoration'), where he taught classes and also promoted the martial arts.

When he turned forty-seven, he decided to pass the lordship of Hirado to his son. Obviously, he was not very interested in nor did he enjoy being the lord. In fact, he spent all his time afterward writing and training in the martial arts. He took on the pen name *Seizan* (静山) and started writing the previously mentioned *Kasshi Yawa* in 1821. It was his daily task to

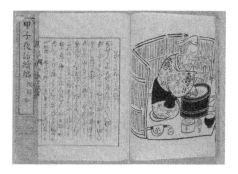

write something to add to this collection of essays every night until his last days. By the end, the book had grown to contain 278 volumes.

I mentioned earlier that Matsuura lived in the peaceful part of the Edo period. In other words, there was much less demand on the samurai with regard to the martial arts. For this reason, it was natural that they would focus their time on literary education and other arts, such as the tea ceremony, music, and songs. Matsuura, on the other hand, spent much of his time on the martial arts. At the same time, he continued to write his essays. Since he was self-taught, I am pretty sure one of the things he studied was the military strategies of the ancient Chinese expert in this area, Sun Tzu (孫子, 544 BC–496 BC).

Sun Tzu was not only a general and a tactician but also a writer and a philosopher. He is known mostly for his famous book, *The Art of War* (published in the fifth century BC). Most readers probably know, or at least have heard, that this military strategy book had a huge influence on Western and Asian military philosophy.

I have read this book (in Japanese), and I learned a lot from it. Here I wish to share the top-ten famous quotes by Sun Tzu. Reading these quotes may not tell you exactly which ones gave Matsuura his ideas, but I think they are beneficial to all *karateka* as I am sure they will teach something to all of us. Here are three of the most famous quotes:

- If you know the enemy and know yourself, you need not fear the results of a hundred battles.
- All men can see these tactics whereby I conquer, but what none can see is the strategy out of which victory is evolved.
- Thus, what is of supreme importance in war is to attack the enemy's strategy.

The following seven quotes may not have had a direct impact on Matsuura's quote, but I am sharing them here as I believe they can give us much wisdom in the martial arts. I believe these are fairly straightforward; thus, I am sure any comments or explanations I might have would not add much value to them. One thing I can say is that the ideas shown below are beneficial to both practitioners and instructors.

- He will win who knows when to fight and when not to fight.
- Be extremely subtle, even to the point of formlessness. Be extremely mysterious, even to the point of soundlessness. Thereby you can be the director of the opponent's fate.
- The general who advances without coveting fame and retreats without fearing disgrace, whose only thought is to protect his country and do good service for this sovereign, is the jewel of the kingdom.
- To fight and conquer in all our battles is not supreme excellence; supreme excellence consists in breaking the enemy's resistance without fighting.
- The art of war teaches us to rely not on the likelihood of the enemy's not coming but on our own readiness to receive him, not on the chance of his not attacking but rather on the fact that we have made our position unassailable.
- A good commander is benevolent and unconcerned with fame.
- Regard your soldiers as your children, and they will follow you into the deepest valleys; look upon them as your own beloved sons, and they will stand by you even unto death.

I believe I have given enough information about the author and his background. By now, you are probably becoming impatient and worried that I will never give an explanation of his quote. Don't worry. I will get into this right now.

Believe it or not, this quote was not too popular in Japan until recently. In fact, it became well known to us only when a famous professional baseball manager, Katsuya Nomura (野村克也, 1935–2020), used it to explain his baseball philosophy. I will not get sidetracked by introducing Mr. Nomura in this chapter. His background is not really relevant to the quote, so I will only say that he was a famous baseball player in the sixties and seventies who later became a successful manager and was inducted into the Japanese Baseball Hall of Fame in 1989. Again, what is really important about Nomura is that he brought this quote back from history. Without him, it would have been remembered only by historians and kenjutsu buffs. It is very possible that we *karateka* would not have learned about it.

To understand the essence of this saying, we need to study the literal meaning first. The first half, *kachi ni fushigi no kachi ari*, has the word *kachi* (勝ち) twice, and this word means 'victory', 'win', or 'winning'. *Fushigi* (不思議) means 'mystery'. The last word, *ari* (有り), means 'exists' or 'is possible'. The other words, *ni* (に) and *no* (の), are grammatical particles.

When all of the words are put together, this clause means 'in victory, there is a mysterious victory'. In other words, when you win, you may find your victory to be mysterious. So, in some victories, you do not know how you won despite the fact that you may know exactly how you won in many other cases. And, on some occasions, though you expected to lose, you may end up winning and just not know how it happened.

Have you personally experienced or witnessed something like this? I do not watch sports, so I do not follow the stats. However, I remember that there was a big upset when the Japanese soccer team beat the Colombian soccer team in the 2018 FIFA World Cup. Japan had almost zero chance of winning, and no one expected them to win, but, to everyone's surprise, they actually won. It was a *fushigi no kachi*, a mysterious victory.

GOALS and HIGHLIGHTS
COLOMBIA vs JAPAN (1 - 2)

Even if you do not know how you won, a win is a win. However, instead of just being happy about it, you should investigate why a victory was possible. Even though it may seem mysterious at first, by knowing the opponent and yourself better, you may be able to discover why it happened. The reason may lie in your effort. You might have practiced much more than the opponent. Or, it may be due to the fault of the opponent. Maybe he was not in good health or the right mental condition and did not play at 100%. By finding out the exact reasons, you may be able to repeat the victory in your next fight. However, you must never become conceited or overconfident. Such an attitude will surely lead to defeat in the future.

OK, let's look at the second clause. In *make ni fushigi no make nashi*, we have two instances of the word *make* (負け). As you might suspect, this word means 'defeat', 'loss', or 'losing'. We have already gone over *fushigi* (不思議), which, again, means 'mystery'. The final word, *nashi* (なし), is the opposite of *ari* (あり), and it means 'does not exist' or 'is impossible'. The remaining words are the same grammatical particles as before.

When all of the words are put together, this clause means 'in defeat, there is no mysterious defeat'. In other words, when you lose, there is no mystery as to why you lost. When you lose in a battle or a fight, you can always find the reason for your loss. There is an excellent example of this in Japan's going to war with

the U.S. in 1941 and then losing that war in 1945. At the time the war began, the official GDP of the U.S. was more than triple that of Japan. However, in reality, the economic size of the U.S. was at least seven times, and possibly ten times, greater than that of Japan.

In addition, we can compare some of the necessary industrial capacities. According to the statistics given by *The Pacific War Online Encyclopedia*, Japan's production of crude oil in 1941 was only a little over 5 million barrels (http://pwencycl.kgbudge.com/O/i/Oil.htm). That of the U.S., on the other hand, was almost 500 million barrels according to the Railroad Commission of Texas (www.rrc.texas.gov/oil-and-gas/research-and-statistics/production-data/historical-pro-

duction-data/crude-oil-production-and-well-counts-since-1935/). You can easily
see that U.S. crude-oil production was nearly a hundred times that of Japan.

The production of steel in Japan in
1941 was about 6.5 million tons according to Richard Krause's Master of
Arts thesis entitled "The Iron and Steel
Industry in Wartime Japan, 1931–
1945" (https://shareok.org/bitstream/
handle/11244/23634/Thesis-1972-K91i.pdf). U.S. steel production, on the other
hand, was 387 million tons between 1941 and 1945. If you divide that figure by
5, the annual production can be estimated to be a little under 80 million tons. Unfortunately, I could not find a U.S. source for this information. The source I have
is from a 1967 NKK article (www.jstage.jst.go.jp/article/jie1922/47/1/47_1_43/
pdf/-char/ja).

There are many other statistics to prove that Japan was not a viable match
for the U.S. Despite this fact, Japan declared war and ended up in total defeat
after four years. This was a foolish war to engage in, and there was certainly no
mystery in the defeat.

Some Japanese, including some historians, tend to blame bad luck or something other than the obvious reasons. Many say Japan won the spiritual war or
the battle of the mind but lost because of the number of weapons, such as planes
and battleships. They do not wish to blame their faulty decision-making. Blaming
someone or something else is much easier. But, in the end, it is only an excuse
and will not help you. If you are not honest with yourself and do not discover the
real reason you lost, you may repeat the same mistakes in the next fight or battle.

For instance, if you happen to be sick or out of shape on the day of a match
or fight, and you lose, you could say, "It was bad luck that I got sick on that day."
Then, if you forget about it, you may get sick again on another event day. This
may happen because you did not look more deeply and more seriously into yourself and your life.

Check your sleeping habits. Maybe you did not sleep well or sleep enough. How were your eating habits? You might not have eaten right or might have eaten too much. Your sickness might have had a psychological cause. Maybe you became extremely tense or nervous, and the heavy mental strain affected your physical condition. By studying every aspect of yourself, you may be able to find the exact cause of the sickness you experienced on the important day of your match.

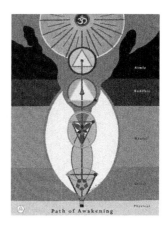

Conclusion

As you have seen, this quote consists of two parts. It describes not only a winning situation but also a losing situation, which I think makes it a valuable quote. It is rather short. Matsuura does not give an explanation in his essay. It is almost as if he were throwing it at us and challenging us to find the meaning on our own. On the surface, the statement is more like a baffling Zen question. For many, it can be very puzzling, and its meaning can be invisible. For some, it may bring no message of deep meaning. However, you can find the essence of martial-arts wisdom once you come to a full understanding of the truth hidden in this short statement. To be able to understand this completely, I think we must have some intense training behind us, both mental and physical, in order to back up our thinking.

CHAPTER NINE
第九章

HOW KARATE STARTS WITH AN UKE
受けで始まるとは？

Have you heard your sensei tell you that in karate, the
very first movement, whether in *kata* or *kumite*, is an
uke (受け, 'block')? Well, at least I have. For many
years, I did not doubt it or even contemplate it. Now
that I have a better understanding of karate techniques,
I may have a deeper understanding of this statement. I
am happy that I can share it here in this short chapter.

Karate was created hundreds of years ago on Okinawa, and if you are familiar with its history, you will know that Okinawa was a kingdom for many years. There was a place in the capital, Shuri, where many samurai protected their king. In addition to their standard weapons, such as swords and spears, they adopted a hand-to-hand combat method. Though there was an influence from Chinese fighting systems, the Okinawan samurai created their own unique fighting method and called it *te* (手, 'hand'). This is what is now known as *karate* (空手, 'empty hand').

Therefore, we agree that karate is a form of *budo*. This means karate is an art that is designed to kill the opponent or enemy. But, times have changed, and an empty-handed combat system would seem to be outdated. Despite this, however, karate grew to become one of the greatest activities of the twentieth century, and it is expected to grow even more as it was even included in the 2021 Olympic Games.

When you look at recent history, you will note that all martial arts were banned by General Headquarters (GHQ) at the end of World War II. In order to revive karate, Funakoshi had to say that karate was an art of self-defense only. And, to prove that it was not an aggressive art, he had to say that the first move in every karate technique was a block.

Some karate practitioners still believe that one of the reasons we start with an *uke* is that karate is not a vicious fighting method and is an art that is for self-defense only. For this reason, practitioners refrain from attacking first and instead wait until the opponent or enemy strikes. In fact, many of them cite a famous Funakoshi saying, *Karate ni sente nashi* (空手に先手無し, 'There is no first attack in karate'), as a proof of their claim. Though this was created by Funakoshi, even practitioners of styles other than Shotokan seem to share this concept.

In fact, for many years, I was a believer in this and had no doubt about it. However, as I have studied karate more, I have begun to understand that there is much more to it than the simple reason mentioned above. In fact, many practitioners misunderstand what Funakoshi wanted to tell us, but it becomes clearer once you understand the true concept of this statement.

First of all, we need to examine the Japanese word *uke* (受け). It is translated as the noun 'block'. However, it can also refer to the act of catching or receiving. For 'to catch a baseball', we say, "*Boru o ukeru*" (ボールを 受ける). In judo and jujutsu, many different

kinds of techniques for softening a fall have been developed and practiced. These techniques are called *ukemi* (受け身, literally, 'catching the body'). Here, *uke*

UKEMI WAZA

USHIRO UKEMI

ZEMPO KAITEN UKEMI

YOKO UKEMI

MAE UKEMI

refers to the concept of receiving or softening the impact of landing on the floor when you are being thrown. These meanings, I think, are very interesting. As you can see, the concept behind them is not confrontational; rather, it has to do with going along with something or diverting it. When you block in karate, maybe you want to have a feeling of catching or diverting the opponent's attack and leveraging his power to your advantage.

Regardless of how you block an attack, do you think it is wise and advantageous to always wait in a real fight? Many war strategists disagree. You may remember that there is another famous saying, which is *Sente hissho* (先手必勝, 'First attack guarantees victory'). This is not an original karate saying. It came from other Japanese martial arts. In fact, this concept was also adopted in sports and other competitions, including games such as *shogi* (将棋, '[Japanese] chess') and *igo* (囲碁), or *go* (碁 [photo right]). This concept is the complete opposite of what Funakoshi stated.

When I was faced with these two martial-arts sayings some forty to forty-five years ago, I got confused. I certainly could not explain how these two opposite concepts could be correct in karate. This confusion motivated me to investigate not only the in-depth meaning of the sayings but also the history of karate and Okinawa. I wrote about the apparent contradiction between these two sayings in Chapter 13: "Contradiction in 'Karate ni Sente Nashi' and 'Sente Hissho?'" of my book *Shotokan Myths*. If you are interested in this subject and wish to read more about it, I suggest you read that chapter. In this chapter, I will provide further information on this subject.

First, let's look at a few ancient Chinese philosophies on this subject.

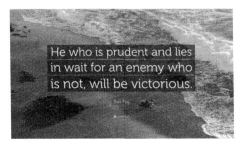

He who is prudent and lies in wait for an enemy who is not, will be victorious.

The first one is the famous strategy book *The Art of War* by Sun Tzu. The following statement is very relevant to our discussion: *Sakinjite senchi ni orite, teki o matsu mono wa issu* (先んじて戦地に処りて、敵を待つものは佚す, 'He who is prudent and lies in wait for an enemy who is not will be victorious'). This means that when engaging in combat, the force that occupies the key terrain first will gain a decisive advantage over the force that arrives late. The force that reaches the key terrain later will be at a disadvantage because it has to fight immediately. This means that force will not be able to prepare or do reconnaissance. The soldiers will not get any rest or downtime before battle. Thus, you can see the obvious advantage to being ready first.

Here is another one. The Han dynasty official and historian Qian Sima (司馬遷, c. 145 BC–86 BC) published a very famous Chinese book entitled *Records of the Grand Historian* (c. 91 BC). This book is a comprehensive history of ancient China comprising 130 chapters

and totaling over 520,000 words. In this book is the teaching *Sakinzureba hito o seisu* (先んずれば人を制す, 'If you go ahead of others, you will get the better of them').

It is true that ancient wisdom seems to vouch for the Japanese saying *Sente hissho*. I have also studied the strategies of Napoleon Bonaparte (1769–1821) and Niccolò Machiavelli (1469–1527). I will not quote their statements, but both of them believed in a similar concept. In addition, we already know the concept that the best defense is a good offense as this statement is frequently used in football and basketball games. I even found an obscure English saying: *The foremost dog catches the hare*.

I have listed many beliefs and concepts above that support *Sente hissho*. If this is the case, then waiting for an opponent to strike first does not seem like a wise choice or strategy. Then, why did Funakoshi tell us that all karate techniques start with an *uke*? Does this mean all that ancient wisdom was incorrect? It is hard to believe that. Thus, I have come to realize that these opposing ideas are simply two sides of the same coin.

I believe this is a very interesting subject that we need to look at and evaluate closely. I would like to show you that the reverse can be true and very enlightening.

In the Japanese games of *shogi* and *go*, there is a belief in *Sente hissho*. This means that the person who makes the first move is considered to be at an advantage. This is true in

a game, but it is not always applicable in a fight or battle. In a chess game, the players are both prepared and have much time to think about their strategy before they make the next move. In a fight, on the other hand, there is little to no time to think once it starts.

The reality of the English saying *The foremost dog catches the hare* is that the first dog does not necessarily catch the prey. For instance, one dog may be the first one to jump on the prey, but he may miss and not catch it. In this case, it is possible that the second or even the third dog may indeed catch the hare. Being there first will definitely give you an advantage, but it does not guarantee the result. So, the saying covers only the part about the advantage but does not say anything about the result.

Ancient wisdom tells us that we need to be there and be ready first. What we have to be careful about is not mixing up this idea with the concept of attacking first. In fact, an opponent who attacks first can put himself at a disadvantage. By revealing his first move to you, he allows you to read his tactics; thus, you can act accordingly. You may follow up with a counterattack that your opponent may not expect. You need to be ready mentally, but you should wait until the opponent commits to an action that will put you in an advantageous situation. This condition that is described as being the first move is an *uke*, an act of catching. Now it makes sense that the actual technique may not necessarily be a block. Rather, it just means that you will be on the receiving or catching side.

Let me add that what I have described above, that is, not throwing the first attack, does not guarantee an advantage every time. This may sound contradictory, and you may be confused. I should explain further to clarify this point for those who might not have understood clearly.

If the first attack you execute is unexpected or invisible, you have a much greater chance of defeating your opponent. In other words, if the opponent is not mentally or physically prepared for your first attack, he will definitely be at a disadvantage.

Here is a tactic. When you are totally prepared for any action, including an attack or a block, this status itself will force the opponent to execute the first attack. He will most likely do so when he is not completely ready. In this situation, you will be on the *uke* (receiving) side, but you are at an advantage. You can easily react properly to the first move made by the opponent that puts him at a disadvantage.

I jokingly tell my students that it is like the children's game Rock Paper Scissors. The guy who sticks his hand out later can always win as he can see the

other guy's hand. Yes, this is cheating in the game, but it can be a wise tactic in a street fight. However, it definitely requires total preparation and the ability to react properly to the opponent's first move. How can you do this?

The short answer is *train*. Yes, it will require much training. This is why you need to train every day, and not just in the dojo. Your training must extend into your daily-life activities, such as standing, sitting, walking down the street, driving a car, riding a bicycle, etc.

Conclusion

The ancient Okinawan *te* masters reached expert levels where they could be ahead of the normal advantage. They allowed their opponents to have the advantage of attacking first, but, in the end, this would work against the opponents. In other words, they could read the minds and tactics of their opponents. They might have looked as though they were just blocking an attack. However, in some cases, that block could be so strong that it might discourage the opponent from attacking further. The experts could stay within the attacking range and yet still keep the opponent from touching them. They could execute these effective counters (*uke*) every time because they were at an advantage.

This is exactly where you should be and what Funakoshi and the ancient experts want you to achieve. You want to train and reach the stage where every movement of your karate starts with an *uke*.

I want to end this chapter with an interesting kanji fact that may be very enlightening to some people. I already showed the kanji for *uke* earlier (illustration below left). Now I will show you another kanji next to it (illustration below right). This one is pronounced *ai*, and it means 'love'. They look very similar, don't they? Isn't that interesting?

Love

As you can see, there is an extra part in the middle of the kanji for *ai*. That part is *kokoro* (心 [illustration right]), which is, in fact, a stand-alone character. Some readers may already know this, but *kokoro* means 'heart'. So, the character for 'heart' is placed in the

middle of the character for *uke*, and this turns it into the character for 'love'. We certainly do not block our heart in order to obtain love. We must open our heart instead. We give and receive love. Here we can also see the true meaning of *uke*. It refers to receiving and also to giving. In other words, an *uke* absorbs the attack and returns the energy to the opponent. In this way, an *uke* nullifies the attack. What do you think?

CHAPTER TEN
第十章

THE MYSTERY OF IRIMI
入り身の不思議

This term, *irimi* (入り身), is frequently used in aikido. In fact, it is considered to be one of this martial art's most important technical concepts. Morihei Ueshiba (植芝盛平, 1883–1969 [photo below]), the founder of aikido, wrote his belief on page 163 of his book *Aikido Shinzui* (合気道神髄 [Hachiman Shoten, 2002]): "入り身転換の法を会得すれば、どんな構えでも破っていける." This translates as 'If you master the law of *irimi tenkan*, you can break through any posture', which means that you can fight off any attack.

In fact, I believe this is an important technical concept not only for aikido but also for karate. This is especially so for Asai Ryu karate as its fundamental techniques are based on *irimi* and *tenshin* (転身). Unfortunately, this concept does not seem to be so popular and is not often practiced in modern-day karate. I hope this chapter will provide the reader with some understanding on this important subject.

The term *irimi* consists of two Japanese words: *iri* (入り) and *mi* (身). Let's look at the meaning of these words. *Iri* means 'entering'; *mi* means 'body'. Thus, the compound term literally means 'entering body', referring to how our body enters or steps forward. Of course, based just on the explanation I've given so far, the meaning is still unclear. Let's look further in order to understand the concept expressed by this term more deeply.

Irimi is a popular technique that is used regularly in aikido. As the opponent moves toward you, instead of moving away, you step toward him. Since this concept comes from aikido, we need to touch on another aikido technique that is called *tenkan* (転換). *Ten* (転) means 'turn' or 'rotate', and *kan* (換) means 'replace' or 'change'. This compound term, then, means 'conversion'. So, this technique has to do with converting the opponent's actions in a way that is to your advantage. Now you understand better why Ueshiba stated that the ultimate aikido techniques are *irimi* and *tenkan*.

Interestingly, many *irimi* and *tenkan* techniques exhibit the popular Asian concept of yin and yang, which represent cosmic duality, that is, sets of two op-posing but complementary principles. The first term, *yin* (陰), which is read as *yīn* in Chinese and *in* in Japanese, means 'darkness' or 'shad-ow'. You could also say that it represents the negative. The other term, *yang* (陽), on the other hand, which is read as *yáng* in Chinese and *yo* in Japanese, means 'light' or 'brightness', so it could also be said to represent the positive.

Thus, the *tenkan* and *irimi* techniques represent yin and yang. The *tenkan* motion of turning or rotating is yin. The *irimi* motion of entering or stepping in is yang. By the way, this concept of yin and yang is very interesting but very com-plex. I plan to write a chapter on this subject, and I promise that a full explana-tion will be included in that future publication.

In basic *irimi* training for karate use, you step forward either toward the twelve-o'clock position or at an angle. After stepping in, you end up with your body facing the attacker rather than facing the direction of the step. If your back is to the opponent, you will need to turn or rotate quickly to face the opponent. This rotating motion is called *tenkan* in aikido. In Asai Ryu karate, we call it *ten-shin*; thus, I will use the latter term, if necessary, to describe body rotation.

Timing is critical to the execution of *irimi*. You need to move in at the very moment of the attack. As you become more capable of controlling distance, you may not need to move too much. However, in this chapter, we will focus only on the technique of stepping forward. I have practiced judo but never aikido. Thus, I am an amateur when it comes to aikido techniques. However, when I have ob-served some of the aikido experts, such as Gozo Shioda (塩田剛三, 1915–1994) and Morihiro Saito (斎藤守弘, 1928–2002), I have noticed that their techniques, particularly their footwork, look very much like those of Asai Ryu karate.

OK, let us move on. I understand that the *irimi* principle is very common to most aikido movements. To understand *irimi* better, we need to study some aikido concepts and techniques. The *kamae* (構え, 'postures') and movements of aikido typically utilize diagonal stances. A popular one is *shumoku dachi* (撞木

立ち), or *shumoku ashi* (撞木足), which looks like the karate stance *re no ji dachi* (レの字立ち), but, interestingly, the front foot points outward, which is the opposite of what we do in karate.

I also understand that these stances were adapted from sojutsu, but I will not go into the explanation of them as they are not directly related to *irimi*. What is important and interesting here is that aikido stances favor the oblique direction.

Irimi movement certainly brings your body very close to that of your opponent. This means that you place yourself in a position relative to the opponent where he cannot maximize his attacks. This is very obvious in a *kumite* situation. When the opponent is too close, most practitioners do not know how to punch or kick, even though most of them have learned short-distance techniques, such as *kagi zuki* (鉤突き), *ura zuki* (裏突き), and elbow strikes.

Anyway, this situation of being too close results in a unique defensive technique because you are able to get into a sort of safe harbor where you can divert the opponent's attacks. On the other hand, it is scary for many practitioners

to get into this position. This causes them to hesitate or to step aside instead of forward. In addition, you will receive an attack if you fail to deliver an effective counterattack immediately.

According to aikido, there are three different *irimi* stages, which I find very interesting. Here is the essence of the three stages:

1. When your opponent's and your separate forces are pushing against each other, you guide the flow of the combined forces in the natural direction.
2. When the opponent attacks, you shift quickly to his blind side.
3. Before the opponent attacks, you execute *irimi* while guiding him to step in.

Now allow me to further explain these three stages of progression in mastering the *irimi* technique.

The first stage is to feel the resistance of the physical force between you and the opponent, which is called *physical-force clash*. Then, change the direction of the force while resisting. Finally, lean your body in and enter.

The second stage is to clash with the force within the opponent. Feel a sense of pressure from him. Push back on the pressure nonphysically to wrap him up. Lean in to the other side of him and enter.

The final stage is to be conscious of space. Create space between you and your opponent. Mentally squeeze the space or eliminate it. Then, guide the opponent in the direction you wish. When mastered, you hardly need to move to execute this technique. As a result, the opponent appears to have missed the intended direction and attacked an empty space.

OK, up to now, I have explained what aikido says about *irimi*. I am hoping that you have gotten a good idea what *irimi* is or can be. Then, you may ask, "Do we really need it?" I am aware that *irimi* is neither taught nor practiced in *kumite* situations in most karate dojo. You may feel you do not need it. I hope you will read this entire chapter so that you can come to your own conclusion and the answer to the above question.

When an opponent attacks you—in other words, when he shortens the dis-

 tance—it is almost natural for you to step back or move away from the attack so that you can maintain the distance. This is true for amateurs and unskilled *karateka* as stepping straight back is probably the worst option in fighting. I do not need to explain why. If a car were coming toward you, would you run backward? You could save your own life by stepping sideways to dodge the car.

Well, the concept is the same in karate as you wish to dodge a charging opponent. We only teach white belts to step back toward the six-o'clock position because it utilizes the easiest footwork. But, as you advance in skill and achieve intermediate *kyu* levels, we teach you to step back toward the four- and eight-o'clock positions, and then we teach you to step laterally toward the three- and nine-o'clock positions. As you advance even further in your technique, you will need to learn how to step in toward the opponent. I realize that this sounds counterintuitive, and this is why *irimi* is for advanced practitioners.

When you see a truck or bus coming toward you, I am not telling you to walk toward it. This works only in martial-arts situations. In other words, you are not fighting a truck or a bus. You just need to dodge it in order to save yourself, and that is the end of the story. However, in the case of fighting, just dodging a punch or a kick will not be the end. The opponent will continue to attack you unless you somehow stop him or his attacks. This means you need to counterattack by executing a punch, kick, or throw. Chokes and joint locks are other possibilities, but this is not too effective unless you are very skillful with these techniques.

Now you may still have a nagging question: why do we want to step in? As I explain the reasons, you will understand why this technique is suitable only to the advanced.

Reason 1

The easiest and most visible reason is that shortening the distance between you and the opponent will nullify his attack or render it ineffective. There is, of course, one condition. Shortening the distance must be done correctly. In other words, controlling the distance is a high-level technique itself.

Learning this is not easy. First of all, there is always a fear of doing it. Of course it is scary to move into an attack. You can get rid of this fear only after you learn how to handle this technique skillfully.

Secondly, knowing the correct timing is extremely challenging. If you move too soon or too late, the technique will not work. If you move too soon, the opponent will catch your movement and adjust his attack. If you move too late, he will get you.

Then, you want to know what the correct timing is. It is very difficult to explain in writing, but one thing I can tell you is that the right timing is right after the opponent initiates his attack. He must commit to the move so that he cannot adjust too easily. It is also critical that you make no movement before your *irimi* action. In other words, your opponent must never be able to predict your movement. It must be a total surprise to him.

Another challenge of the *irimi* technique is the short distance itself. As you step in toward the opponent and he moves in toward you at the same time, the distance is shortened. In this case, using your blocks and/or counterattacks becomes extremely difficult. You need to be able to judge the distance, and you also need to know how to apply the techniques from that short distance.

Shotokan karate is a long-distance fighting method, so this is even more challenging for Shotokan practitioners. It may be easier for practitioners of short-distance fighting methods, such as Goju Ryu and Wing Chun (詠春), to handle this distance and deliver the techniques effectively. However, it is still challenging even for them to judge the ever-changing distance.

Reason 2

By stepping in toward the opponent, you may
be able to position yourself in a blind spot, which is
a major advantage over the opponent.

The correct positioning of yourself during and
after *irimi* is very tricky and challenging. Many
fail at the technique because they run into the opponent. Even if you miss your opponent, you may
not end up in a position or angle where you can apply the techniques properly or
effectively.

Reason 3

As you step in, the forward movement will increase the power of your technique. If you move away from the opponent, however, you lose power. Just think
of the concept of two cars running into each other. The damage to the cars is
much greater than if a moving car hits a stationary one.

There are a few challenging points here.

Firstly, you need to be able to control
that increased power and leverage it within
your technique. If you cannot control it,
your technique will be wild and may be
rendered ineffective.

Secondly, you need to apply the technique while you are still moving, either
forward or in rotation. Applying a technique or a combination from a stationary
stance is obviously much easier than doing it while you are in motion.

Thirdly, you need to apply the technique while the opponent is also still
moving. It is almost like two partners dancing. In aikido, this condition is called

musubi (結び), which means 'merging' or 'union'. In other words, you must almost blend your movements into those of the opponent. By doing so, you can add his power to yours. When you watch a pair of excellent dancers, you can see that they are aiding each other with their individual moves. Thus, they look not only graceful but also dynamic and powerful.

Wouldn't it be wonderful if your *kumite* with your opponent could look like a dance of death?

CHAPTER ELEVEN
第十一章

ATERU WAZA
A "FORGOTTEN" TECHNIQUE
当てる技
忘れられた技術

In this chapter, I plan to present one serious but unnoticed or forgotten problem in modern-day karate training. What I am referring to is a diluted or misdirected objective in the *kumite* training found in most traditional dojo. I consider this to be very serious and wish more people would pay attention to it. However, not too many practitioners even care to know about it.

Lately, karate has been enjoying lots of popularity. Sport karate even became more popular after the event in the 2021 Tokyo Olympics. So, naturally, not only karate practitioners but also many instructors must be very happy about the positive influence from the Olympics. I suspect they believe karate is progressing well and is even advancing.

I am a *budo karateka*; thus, I am seriously concerned. I am not simply opposed to karate's being included in the Olympics. It is a more deep-seated problem than that. I am afraid the current trend will ruin the *budo*, or true karate, that was handed down from our forefathers for many centuries. The popularity we are seeing lately is actually a process to make karate a useless or ineffective martial art.

Let me share a Japanese saying: *kiba o nuita tora* (牙を抜いた虎). *Kiba* means 'fangs'. *Nuita* means 'pulled out'. Many people may already know this, but *tora* means 'tiger'. Therefore, the whole saying means 'a tiger with its fangs pulled out'. This is very similar to the Western saying *paper tiger*, so I do not need to explain further. In fact, sport karate is a sports event (a paper tiger) and cannot be considered a martial art (a tiger that still has its fangs).

OK, enough of the introduction. Now I need to further explain the subject itself. I am referring to a technique that is called *ateru gijutsu* (当てる技術) or *ateru waza* (当てる技) in Japanese. It literally means 'target-hitting technique'. I am sure you will agree that an attacking technique, whether punching or kicking, is ineffective if it misses the target. It does not matter how fast or strong that technique may be. It is wasted.

I suspect you have experienced in your *kumite* training that it is difficult to

HITTING THE TARGET

land your attacking techniques on a precise target. I also assume you have experienced that your techniques are either too far from or too close to the target. This is a technical problem, and it can be solved if proper training is implemented and practiced. So, you may ask, "Then, what is the problem here?"

OK, let me explain. I am aware that the problem is not very obvious. So, we must go beyond what it seems to be superficially. I will cover the reasons we have these problems and how we can solve them as we progress through this chapter. I hope to reveal the core problem that sits deep inside traditional karate.

Regarding hitting a target, we must first cover the important subject of the targets themselves. Since most readers already know what the targets are in *kumite*, they may think it is unnecessary to discuss this topic. Though it may seem unimportant, it really is an important topic to discuss.

Targets

This is an important subject as I understand that most karate students do not learn what the true targets are. You may consider my statement to be nonsense or groundless. I am aware that you have learned what the targets are from your teacher and that you are very clear about them in your *kumite* training. They are, of course, *jodan* (上段), *chudan* (中段), and *gedan* (下段).

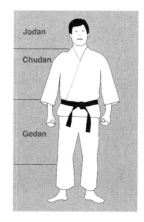

Here is an illustration of the target areas you learn about in your karate training. You will most likely agree that *jodan* refers to any part above the neckline, *chudan* is the area between the neckline and the belt, and *gedan* is the whole area below the belt but typically refers to the groin. It looks very simple and clear, so we don't see any problems here.

Unfortunately, the very understanding of these targets themselves is technically incorrect, or, at the best, inaccurate. More importantly, we sadly lack an understanding and appreciation of *kyusho* (急所), which are the critical points of the body. I will touch on this subject later in this chapter.

Let me explain the problem by giving some examples of the differences between martial-arts fighting (including street fighting) and the typical *kumite* training conducted at a standard dojo where traditional styles are taught.

For *jodan*, which is at the head level, what do we learn in our *kumite* train-

ing? We are vaguely taught to aim at the face. I am sure you will agree that we do not pay much attention to the details of the *jodan* target. In tournament *kumite*, if your *jodan oi zuki* touches the opponent's nose, or is even in that vicinity, you receive a point.

However, if you are familiar with street fighting or boxing, you know that hitting your opponent in the nose or mouth may not result in a knockout. It may cause a nosebleed. A tooth or two might fall out. But, the opponent will still be standing.

There are other specific spots that are known to produce a knockout. These well-known spots include the area under the chin, the corner of the jaw, and the

temple. If you are a boxing fan, you have seen knockouts and witnessed the effectiveness of these spots in the face and head area. The most common knockout punches in boxing are an uppercut delivered under the chin or a hook punch to the jaw (photo left) or temple. And, in boxing, those are the targets they aim for. Why do we have this difference in our training? We will discover this as our discussion progresses in this chapter.

Let's continue with *chudan*, which is midsection target training. As you will agree, most *chudan* attacks executed by practitioners, as I have observed, are aimed at the general midsection area. This area is well protected by the strong abdominal muscle known as the *rectus abdominis*. There are many critical points in the *chudan* area, such as the solar plexus, the sides of the ribs, the kidney, the armpits, the collarbones, etc. You can see these and other critical spots in the *kyusho* chart shown later. Although it is strange to a *budo* practitioner like me, these precise spots are rarely explained or focused on in the standard *kumite* training that is found in our dojo nowadays.

In addition, we practice *chudan nukite* (中段 貫手, 'middle-level spear hand' [photo right]) in our *kihon* training, and we also find this technique in many Shotokan *kata*, including Heian Nidan (平安二段), Heian Sandan (平安三段), Kanku Dai (観空大), etc. However, this particular technique is rarely used in our *kumite* training. For *chudan*, we almost always use *gyaku zuki* (逆突き, 'reverse punch') or *oi zuki* (追い突き, 'lunge punch') for our arm technique. In fact, even for attacking the *jodan* area, we rarely use open-handed techniques. We will need to discuss why this is so later.

The *gedan* area is even more notable. Though an attack to the groin is effec-

tive, attacking this area is not allowed in tournaments or even in the regular *kumite* training that is found in most dojo. The groin is not the only spot in the *gedan* area. There are other points that are effective in a street fight, which include the knee, the shin, and even the top of the foot.

You know this because you feel great pain when someone stomps on your foot, especially if it is done by a woman in a high-heeled shoe. Kicking the knee from the side or from the rear, as well as from the front when the knee is not bent, certainly causes a great deal of damage to the opponent. Kicking or hitting the shin area also causes great pain.

There are other *kyusho* in the *gedan* area, but I will not list them here as I feel I have listed enough examples. Once again, all these areas of the lower half of the body (the area below the hips) are taught very little in most dojo. Even if these spots are taught in your dojo, your sensei most likely does not allow you to attack them in your *kumite* training.

Up until now, I have illustrated that the targets we refer to in our *kumite* are, at best, vague and that they are, in fact, inaccurate or even incorrect. Many of us lack the knowledge of the critical spots and of the correct (and real) distancing in our *kumite* training.

OK, I believe I have spent enough time on the problems relating to the targets in our *kumite* training. Now we must ask, "Why do we have this problem?" There are two structural and fundamental reasons for these "flaws," which are (1) sport karate and (2) the concept of *sundome*.

Sport Karate

The term *sport karate* does not refer only to tournament karate. The problem does not stop there. It includes our regular dojo *kumite* training because, in most cases, we must perform *kumite* under certain rules or restrictions. Tournament

kumite has even more restrictions and limitations. This means practitioners are prohibited from executing many techniques, such as kicking the groin area or poking the eyes, for instance. There are many other techniques that are prohibited, and I do not think I need to list them all here as I am sure you know what they are.

I find it ironic that those techniques are considered to be "too dangerous" and are thus prohibited for safety reasons. Isn't karate supposed to be the martial art for killing? I see a contradiction here. We old-timers used to talk about throwing our punches according to the concept of *ikken hissatsu*. Unfortunately, this concept seems to be long forgotten now.

Let's look at modern-day sport karate. It has adopted gloves and protectors. But, if we have the *sundome* rule, then there shouldn't be any contact or injuries, right? Theoretically, that is true, and we may wish it were possible. But, in reality, we have discovered that many accidents are encountered in tournament *kumite* situations. Some happen due to overexcitement on the part of the participants, but the biggest reason is that it is extremely difficult for participants to judge the distance between them and their opponents in these fast and continuously moving *kumite* exchanges.

Prohibition of techniques is not just an occurrence that is strictly limited to karate. The unavoidable fact is that permitted targets have to be set as a rule as this is a natural result when a martial art becomes a sport. Kendo, the art of Japanese fencing, is a good example. It has only four permitted targets where you can score a point: *men* (面, 'face'), *do* (胴, 'torso'), *kote* (小手, 'wrist'), and *tsuki* (突き, 'thrust [to the throat]'). This means a kendo practitioner does not receive a point when he hits other parts of the body, such as the arm, shoulder, leg, etc.

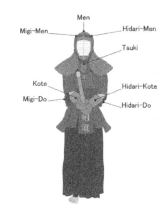

When you think of a fight with a real sword, you realize that cutting the shoulder, arm, or leg of an opponent is a very effective strike. In fact, trying to cut the opponent's shin was one of the most popular attacking techniques of the ancient samurai. You can easily imagine that trying to strike a person's head was less favored as the head is a more challenging target. The opponent's sword is right in front of your face, and the head is where the eyes are located. Thus, you can easily see that the lower part of your body is completely unprotected as it is far from your eyes. Even though attacking the *gedan* area is an effective technique in a real fight situation, it is not included as a legitimate target in kendo.

I could discuss similar situations in judo and kyudo, but I will not do so in this chapter as I think it would be somewhat redundant.

I respect kendo practitioners as they are sincerely trying to preserve the samurai spirit and *bujutsu* in their attitude and spirit. Having said that, I must also say that their techniques, that is, those executed by most practitioners, are no longer realistic or effective from the perspective of real sword fighting. You cannot blame them as this is what rules do. Rules are there to protect the competitors. Otherwise, there would be too many serious injuries, and the art would not be accepted as a sport or in a commercial dojo. The rules are also necessary to make competition itself possible. Without them, it would be a life-or-death match where the loser ends up either maimed or dead. One of these important rules is the definition of targets. By having a clear, agreed-upon definition, points can be scored in matches.

One thing I must add about kendo is that its practitioners have somewhat solved a problem that stems from the second reason, which is addressed below. But, I will not write the details of the solution until after I present the second reason.

Sundome

What is *sundome* (寸止め)? A *sun* (寸) is a unit we use to measure length in Japan. One *sun* is close to one inch. *Tome* (止め) means 'stop'. So, these two terms combined refer to stopping at one inch. In other words, in karate, you need to stop your punch or kick one inch from the target.

Why is this? Obviously, if you allow a punch or kick to land on the target at full force, you will injure your training partner in the dojo or your opponent in a tournament. Certainly, this cannot be allowed. *Karateka* aim to develop a one-punch-one-kill kind of technique. To maintain safety during dojo training, instructors of traditional karate set up this rule.

Then, you may ask, "What is wrong with this rule?" Due to the fact that your punch or kick does not actually hit the target, a few negative things occur.

One is inaccuracy in judging distance. If you continually stop your punch just out of reach of the target, you have trained yourself to miss the target.

Another negative result is the blurring of the precise target. You may have a clear knockout if you hit someone straight on the nose. However, he will most likely not be knocked out if you hit him in the forehead or even in the mouth. But, all of these areas are interpreted as *jodan*, so they are considered to be legitimate targets, and you can score a point when hitting them, regardless of the difference in effectiveness.

I can think of one funny but serious consequence of the *sundome* rule. This happens when you are very close to the opponent. In this situation, it is obviously quite difficult to execute an effective *jodan* attack. In a few dojo, I have witnessed instructors teaching their students to "punch through" with their *jodan* punch. In fact, they teach the students to punch and extend their arm next to the opponent's head.

Yes, in this manner, you can punch very powerfully, and you can extend your punching arm fully. You also feel good as you imagine—falsely, I might add— that you have punched through your opponent's head. I must say that whether or not this training method is beneficial or helpful is highly debatable. Regardless, what you are taught to do is simply punch the air next to the opponent's head.

This means you train to miss the target on purpose, and, for this reason, I strongly oppose this training method.

Now we need to ask why we have these problems. It does not stem from poor training alone. The sad part of the problem is that few *karateka* realize there even is a serious problem. It is also unfortunate that not too many instructors know how to fix the problem even if they find the causes. Regardless, we need to know the causes to understand the problem better. Later, I hope to propose some solutions to these problems.

I have already explained that in order to avoid serious physical injury, the traditional karate styles adopted a noncontact system. This potential problem can be even more serious when it comes to kenjutsu. The danger of using a real sword when you practice with your partner is very obvious here.

One solution can be found in kendo, whose practitioners wear a full protector, known as *bogu* (防具), and use a bamboo sword, called a *shinai* (竹刀), instead of

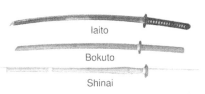

Iaito

Bokuto

Shinai

a real sword. With these tools, they can theoretically hit the opponent as hard as they wish. In other words, they do not need to stop their technique before it lands on the opponent.

They seem to have solved this problem. On the other hand, this change brought several shortcomings, as well. I already stated one of them earlier, which was that of the limitations placed on targets. Only four general areas are set up as "legitimate" targets. This is because kendo chose to be a competitive sport, even though it claims to be *budo*.

There is another, potentially a more serious problem. A bamboo sword is nothing like a real sword, not only in weight but also in balance. I have a *shinai*, and I know how light it is. I can swing it easily with one arm. I also had two real katana at one time. Sadly, my parents gave them away without notifying me. They thought it was dangerous to keep them at home. Despite this, I remember how heavy those swords were. A typical *shinai* weighs a little under a pound (around 440 grams), while a sword weighs between two and five pounds (between one and two kilograms), depending on the length. This means a sword can be two to five times heavier than a bamboo stick.

You can easily see the problem here. If you practice only with a *shinai*, you will not learn how to handle a real sword. Secondly, with a *shinai*, you learn to strike but not to cut. I believe there is a huge difference in the nature of the techniques. Thirdly, no matter how strongly you may strike your opponent with a bamboo stick, you are not quite sure and will never know if the attack was fully effective or not. Finally, and the most importantly, by using a bamboo stick and full protective gear, kendo lost the critical sense of danger and fear. This is a very important point that is not often discussed. I will do so later as we find the same problem in karate. Anyway, those are some of the serious problems found in kendo from the perspective of *budo*.

There are many traditional kenjutsu styles and dojo in Japan. They have cho-sen to replace the real sword with a *bokken* (木剣, 'wooden sword'). Even though kenjutsu practitioners train with wooden swords for safety, they have had to adopt the noncontact system (photo right) for the same reason as traditional karate.

Kenjutsu and iaido practitioners maintain a noncontact rule and do not sanction any tournaments. The main difference in training method between kenjutsu and iaido is that in kenjutsu, they practice with an opponent, while in iaido, they mainly practice solo (like practicing *kata* in karate).

The problems found in kenjutsu are very similar to those found in karate's noncontact rule and the weight of kendo's *bokken*. In iaido, they use a real katana, so this part is not a problem. However, they also have the same problem that stems from the noncontact rule as well as the issues with practicing alone. I will not go any further into the nature of these problems here as this chapter is about the problems of traditional karate.

Some people have come up with a few solutions to alleviate the problems of traditional karate. One is a karate style that uses full protectors (photo right), which is called *koshiki karate* (硬式空手, 'hard-style karate'). Even though you can hit or kick with full force, you still have the problem of not knowing or practicing the *kyusho* that are important in the martial arts.

Another problem, as found in kendo, is that you really do not know how effective your technique is because you are wearing full protective gear. The full gear also takes away the fear factor, which I believe is very important. If you are totally protected, then you are not afraid of moving in and taking a chance. Of course, if you get hit first, you will lose the match, but you will most likely not be injured.

There are also full-contact styles, such as Kyokushinkai. Mas Oyama (photo left), the founder of Kyokushinkai, believed the *sundome* rule was wrong. He stated that *sundome* made karate a dance. Kyokushinkai is a knockout style where participants are allowed to punch and kick with full force to most areas with the exception of a few where they are not allowed to hit. Even though you can kick, you are not allowed to punch the head area. You are also prohibited from kicking or punching the groin area. There are a few other prohibitions, but I will not go into those as they are not as important as the ones I have described here.

They say their karate is real *budo* karate. I practiced Kyokushinkai for two years when I was young, so I know how they practice. I agree that their *kumite* is much more realistic and more serious. On the other hand, I did not stay with this style because of a few problems.

The biggest problem I found was that this type of *kumite* cannot be practiced as you get older. It is great when you are in your twenties and possibly thirties. After two years of practicing this style, I became aware of this problem, so I quit. I was practicing Shotokan karate at the same time, so I stayed with Shotokan, where I could continue to practice into my senior years.

The other problem I found in Kyo-kushinkai was that you cannot strike the most vulnerable targets: the face and the groin. As you can see in the photo to the right, these practitioners are at the perfect distance from each other for a punch to the face but are prohibited  from doing this. So, they punch to the *chudan* level, but most of those punches will not knock down the opponent. The *chudan* area is protected by thick muscles and the rib cage, which nullify those attacks. Therefore, they do not practice punching to the face or most of the open-handed techniques. They practice only the techniques that are considered valid in a tournament.

Another thing I did not like and did not considered to be *budo*-like was that the rules they set made it easier for the bigger and stronger guys to win. It was like judo. Because weight works to a competitor's advantage, judo has a weight system, just like boxing. Since Kyokushinkai did not adopt a weight system, the bigger guys definitely have a huge advantage. If it is a martial art, it must be a fighting tool that can be used by smaller people, women, and older people. For these reasons, I do not consider Kyokushinkai to be true *budo* karate.

Despite this, I think both solutions are good, and all *budo*-minded karate practitioners should at least try them in order to enrich their *kumite* experience. You can learn how it feels to hit your opponent with full force and to receive attacks to your body. This experience will most likely cure the problem of being too far with your attacks and counters. Even if the experience does not cure the problem, you will know for sure if your techniques are missing or not reaching the target.

Let us examine traditional karate closely. Those who do not practice Shotokan may not know that, in 1935, Gichin Funakoshi published the book *Karate Do Kyohan* (空手道教範 [Kobunsha, 1935]),
which was the first karate book published in the world and is now considered to be the bible of Shotokan karate. At the end of the book, he added an illustration of all the *kyusho* of the human body (illustration right). It clearly shows more than a few dozen critical spots.

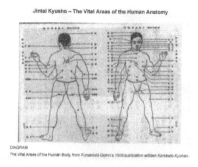

DIAGRAM
The Vital Areas of the Human Body, from Funakoshi Gichin's 1935 publication entitled *Karatedo Kyohan*.

Funakoshi believed karate was *budo* and taught it as such. In fact, he was against having tournaments (sport karate) until his death. He believed that karate should continue to be *budo* and never become a sporting event. Despite his wishes, sport karate became a reality in 1957, the very year he passed.

As we all know, sport karate has become more and more popular in recent years. Let's look further into the problems that have arisen as karate has adopted the *sundome* system and become more of a sport.

Once this became a sporting event governed by rules, *kumite* training in the dojo naturally followed suit with the same rules and principles. As a result, spear-hand techniques, such as eye pokes, were prohibited and thus not practiced. In many dojo these days, practitioners regularly wear light gloves to practice *kumite*. This makes it impossible to use any type of fist other than *seiken* (正拳, 'standard fist'). Sadly, this is how *ipponken* (一本拳), *hiraken* (平拳), and *nakadakaken* (中高拳) had no choice but to disappear from our regular training. And, if a practitioner punches or kicks to the *gedan* area, it is considered a foul, so this technique has also disappeared from our *kumite* training.

Due to all of the facts described above, our typical *kumite* rules had to be reduced to just two targets: *jodan* and *chudan*. You thought the limitation of kendo targets to four areas was bad, but we now have only two targets. As you know, it is that way in tournament *kumite*, as well. You only need to know those two targets or general areas in a match. Thus, knowing the locations of not only the *kyusho* but all other critical points and learning techniques that are not used in tournaments became unimportant or unnecessary in our regular training.

So, I have discussed that not knowing precise and effective targets is one serious flaw of modern-day karate training. I believe I have covered enough on the inaccuracy and vagueness of the targets. We need to move on to the next problem that is also pervasive in our karate training, and I consider this to be even more serious.

Hitting the Target

Even if we know or find the correct target, it is still a problem if we fail to hit it. It does not matter how strong or fast your attacking techniques may be if you miss the target. Moreover, if the blow is weak or the distance is incorrect upon hitting the target, the technique will not be effective or damaging.

I am sure the reader will agree that if your punch is too far from the target or if the impact upon hitting it is too weak, such an attack will have little to none of the desired effect on the opponent. We know that a punch or kick must hit the target in a certain way in order to have an effective (that is, devastating or painful) impact  on the opponent. Distance and power are the two major factors that must be correct in order to produce an effective technique.

It sounds straightforward, and all of us know it, but, at the same time, we also know that it is not that easy to manage. I wonder why this subject is not discussed or taught much. I suspect it is because many instructors do not consider it to be necessary. Therefore, I feel it is my responsibility to discuss this subject here and see if we can find a solution.

First, I must mention that a technique that hits the target accurately and with the proper distance and power requires specific training. Sadly, this type of technique has been forgotten by many and ignored by most simply because we do not see it as necessary. Thus, we train accordingly.

When I talk about landing an attacking technique on a target, *ateru gijutsu*, some of you will quickly think about your hours of training on the *makiwara*. Thus, you may object to my earlier statement and say, "Oh, we punch the *makiwara* every day, so we are practicing hitting a target."

I do not deny the benefits of punching a *makiwara*. Unfortunately, we must realize that *makiwara* training is only a minor part of *ateru gijutsu*. By punching a *makiwara*, you will learn how to strike the target firmly but at a set distance. Most practitioners, however, do not learn how to acquire the correct distance while moving and, at the same time, produce the necessary impact on the target. This happens because the opponent is not a stationary target like a *makiwara*. He is constantly moving and shifting.

In the past, some innovative *karateka* have invented nontraditional karate styles, such as *koshiki karate* (a full-protector system) and Kyokushinkai (a full-contact system). You could try those and see if you feel their approaches are more realistic. However, if you wish to remain within traditional or noncontact karate, here are my suggestions to combat the shortcomings that I have discussed in this chapter. I am sure these suggestions do not cover all of the possible solutions, but they would be a good start.

1. Do not wear protective gear when you practice *jiyu kumite*. This sounds like a drastic suggestion. However, this was the way we used to compete in tournament *kumite* in the seventies and early eighties. You learn

a more realistic distance from targets when you don't wear a face mask, gloves, etc. The other great benefit is the overcoming of the fear of getting really hit. Believe it or not, this factor has not been acknowledged by many. Just think of a situation in which you might be in a street fight. Wouldn't you be better prepared mentally if trained this way? You know my answer.

2. In addition to the *makiwara*, practice with a speed bag and a heavy bag. A speed bag is, of course, for training to hit a target at high speeds. A heavy bag is similar to hitting a human body that is moving but not at high speeds.

3. Practice punching and kicking while closer than the optimum distance of an arm's length away. Before you apply this in your *kumite* practice, you should use a *makiwara* or, better yet, a heavy punching bag that can swing. You need to learn how to generate power while your arm or leg is still bent. You also need to become comfortable fighting at a short distance.

4. Study the *kyusho* and remember them. Then, try to focus on aiming at those specific spots instead of the general *jodan* or *chudan* area during *kumite* practice. As I mentioned above, get used to fighting at a very short

distance from the opponent. In that situation, you must learn effective jamming techniques (that is, short-distance blocking techniques), joint locks, choking, and takedowns in order to execute effective counterattacks at a short distance.

5. Try to touch the opponent when you punch or kick first in *jiyu ippon kumite*. Initially, you want to avoid any contact with the opponent, especially to the *jodan* area, in free sparring. Eventually, you can extend this to that training to develop a keen sense of distance and an ability to

control that distance.

6.   Train with a ball hanging from the ceiling. Initially, you can use a tennis
     ball, which is somewhat large and soft (about
     2½ inches [6.5 centimeters] in diameter), so that
     you can easily punch it. Swing it and hit it while
     you are moving around. Once you get used to
     that, move down to a ping-pong ball (about 1½
     inches [4 centimeters]). The only problem is that
     a ping-pong ball is rather light and does not give
     you the kind of movements you will want. You
     can fill it with sand or water if possible. Eventu-

     ally, get a smaller felt ball of about ¾ inch (2 centimeters) that might be
     commercially available. This training method is, of course, to improve
     your skill at hitting a small target.

7.   When you practice *kihon kumite*, (基本組手, 'basic sparring'), including
     jiyu ippon kumite, be sure to use all parts of the hands and legs. Definite-
     ly include the areas of *nukite* (貫手, 'spear hand'), *teisho* (底掌, 'palm
     heel'), *keito* (鶏頭, 'chicken head'), *kakuto* (鶴頭, 'crane head'), etc.

8.   Be sure to practice attacking and counterattacking the *gedan* area. In
     addition to *gedan*, include all of the other prohibited areas, such as the
     throat and eyes, even though you must be awfully careful when you
     attack those areas. But, this is the reason you need to practice the other
     training methods I listed above in order to develop the technique of judg-
     ing correct distance.

9.   Try not to get too deeply involved in tournaments as a competitor. If you
     are already in them, I have a recommendation that will not be appreciated
     by most instructors and coaches. I dare say that it is best for you to retire
     as soon as possible so that you can practice *budo* karate. You can practice
     sport karate and *budo* karate simultaneously, and many do. Having said
     that, I simply ask why you would want to waste your time and effort in

sport karate if you love *budo* karate, which is the true karate? I may be biased, but that is my honest opinion.

As expected, sport karate will become more mainstream, and instructors will naturally focus on sport-karate techniques and ignore the martial-art way. This means, I am afraid, there will be even fewer *budo karateka* in the future.

However, I am not totally discouraged, nor have I given up hope that there will always be—even if only a small number—some *budo* karate sensei. I believe this because there will always be a few who have discovered the greatness and the benefits of *budo* karate.

That discovery will certainly help you fall in love with the *karatedo*—that is, the true *budo* karate—that was created on Okinawa and handed down to us over several hundred years. I am confident that a chosen few *karateka* will practice the *ateru gijutsu* in order to preserve *budo* karate.

CHAPTER TWELVE
第十二章

WHAT IS THE BEST STANCE?
一番良い立ち方とは？

Though this is a very interesting subject, I am well
aware that this question may be a little too broad
or vague, and your answer will most likely be "It
all depends." The best stance will change, to a
great extent, depending on what martial arts, and
even sporting events, you consider. We also need
to define the meaning of *stance* before we can
jump into this discussion.

As we are, I assume, all *karateka*, we find the
meaning of *stance* to be simple. This term refers
to how we stand. In karate, as you know, we have many stances, such as *zenkutsu
dachi*, *kiba dachi* (騎馬立ち), *neko ashi dachi* (猫足立ち), etc. I am sure you
have your own favorite stance; however, I am not going to limit my discussion
to a specific karate stance. Rather, I wish to talk about the whole posture of the
entire body, including the stance that is used specifically in fighting situations.
We call this *kamae*.

In addition, I am writing this chapter from the perspective of *budo* karate. In
other words, it may not apply to sport karate, tournament karate, or other sporting
events, such as boxing. In this chapter, you will see why this is the case. On the
other hand, it is my belief that the *kamae* I will present in this chapter can apply
to many other martial arts.

So, let's talk about the karate stances first. When you start your karate training, your sensei teaches you different stances as a part of *kihon* training. You start
with the easy ones, such as *shizentai* (自然体, 'natural stance'), and eventually
learn many other stances that are supposedly more advanced. In fact, there are
more than two dozen of them. Each individual stance has its own reason, and you
are told that each one is independently valuable. There is no argument here.

Very interestingly, karate puts more value on having many different stances
than other Japanese martial arts, such as judo, kendo, iaido, jujutsu, etc. It is not
only interesting but also very important that only karate utilizes so many stances.

However, it is not quite related to the subject of this chapter, so we will not discuss this particular point here. Maybe I will write a separate chapter focused on this subject at some other time.

So, we agree that karate has many different stances and that it is very unique for karate
to have so many stances. Then, out of all these
stances, which one do you think is the best for
fighting? Some may say *kokutsu dachi* or *kiba
dachi*, but I suspect many will pick *zenkutsu da-*

chi. I am sure you have a clear reason for which you picked your favorite stance.

I wish to focus on karate; however, I think it is worthwhile to study the stances of other Japanese martial arts, such as aikido, kendo, and judo. The photo below left is of the late aikido master Morihei Ueshiba showing his typical *kamae* with his right foot slightly forward. He is totally relaxed and is extending his right arm forward. The photo below right is from a judo tournament. It shows the beginning of the fight, right after the chief referee says, "*Hajime*!"

There are two photos at the top of the next page. The one on the left shows a couple of kendo practitioners in a standard stance with their right foot forward. They are taught that the right foot should always be forward. I believe this came from the fact that most of us are right handed. The one on the right shows a well-known *kamae* used in Jigen Ryu (示現流) kenjutsu. This kenjutsu style had some impact on the development of Okinawan karate, but we will not discuss this in this chapter. One interesting thing you will notice is that his left foot is placed forward, which is discouraged in kendo.

Since we need to focus on karate stances, I will not evaluate or discuss much on the stances mentioned above. I wanted to share the photos of those *kamae* as reference only. I think they will give us some hints and concepts about *kamae*. We may notice one thing that these photos have in common, however. The stances are rather short, and the knees are not bent. Several of the individuals look as though they were just standing. We will discuss this point later in this chapter.

Before going into karate stances, I wish to touch on one more area. I would like to view the ideas of fighters who are not martial artists. In other words,

what fighting stance do they consider to be the best in a street fight? I think the stance that is shown in the photo to the left is typical. Interestingly, this stance looks similar to our *zenkutsu dachi*, though it is a little high as the legs are almost straight and not bent at the knees. The fighters position their fists high, near or at the face level, to protect that critical area. On the other hand, the lower part of the body (groin, knees, etc.) does not receive much attention. Obviously, this is due to the fact that most street fighters do not engage in kicking or leg techniques.

For the same reason, you will find a very similar stance in boxing. The photo to the right shows Muhammad Ali (1942–2016) on the left in his *kamae* against his opponent on the right. The fist position is high, just as we saw in the street fight. Interestingly, the stance is like *re no ji dachi*, and both fighters have their body weight loaded on their front foot. This is because boxers

shift and change positions much faster and more often than street fighters.

OK, I believe we have spent enough time discussing nonkarate fighting styles. Now let us look closely into the fighting stances of the karate masters.

The photo to the left is of a famous Okinawan master, Choki Motobu (本部朝基, 1870–1944). He visited mainland Japan around the same time Funakoshi started to teach karate in Tokyo. It is recorded that Motobu practiced only a few *kata* and dedicated most of his training to *kumite*. He is known to have engaged in *kakedameshi* (掛け試し), which consisted of street fighting against other karate practitioners, during his youth.

I do not know if the pose shown here was his favorite *kamae*, but I can tell you that his Popeye-sized right arm itself would discourage anyone who might face him. It is certainly scary to me. The stance shown here is very short. It looks like *re no ji dachi* and is interestingly similar to that of Ali shown above.

The photo to the right is of Kenwa Mabuni (摩文仁賢和, 1889–1952), the founder of Shito Ryu. He was known to be very dedicated and was also viewed as a walking encyclopedia of karate since he knew many *kata*. He practiced under Shuri Te (首里手) master Anko Itosu (糸洲安恒, 1831–1915) as well as Naha Te (那覇手) master

Kanryo Higaonna (東恩納寛量, 1853–1915). He also associated with many other karate masters, including Tomari Te (泊手) experts.

This was how he mastered so many different *kata*. In fact, Shito Ryu currently boasts the greatest number of *kata*, which is supposedly either forty-six or forty-seven (including Sansai [サンサイ]). Mabuni might have known even more. He also investigated different methods of *kumite*, including a full-contact style with full protectors.

The stance he assumes here is also interesting as it looks like Shotokan's *kokutsu dachi* or a long version of *re no ji dachi*. What is more interesting to me is how he holds his hands. There is no formal name for this posture. He is obviously showing that he is totally relaxed and can move his hands very quickly to execute whatever technique he may choose.

The photo to the left is of another karate master, Gogen Yamaguchi (山口剛玄, 1909–1989) of Goju Ryu. His nickname was "The Cat" because of his gliding walk and flowing hair. According to an article by Graham Noble on the *Dragon Times* website, Yamaguchi said, "Even today, young man, if you were to face me in combat, I would be able to determine in a second the strength of your ki. Immediately, I would know if you were a good opponent. It is this quality, and no other, which has given me the name of 'The Cat'" (www.dragon-tsunami.org/Dtimes/Pages/articlej.htm).

In this photo he is, of course, assuming *neko ashi dachi*, the cat stance, which is one of the most popular stances of Goju Ryu. Interestingly, *neko ashi dachi*'s foot position is very similar to that of *re no ji dachi*.

Now let's look at two masters within the Shotokai (松濤會), one of the two major organizations based on Funakoshi's style of karate.

The photo at the top of the next page is of the late Shigeru Egami (江上茂, 1912–1981), the founder of the Shotokai. His *kamae* is very unorthodox. Sur-

prisingly, it resembles the *kamae* of aikido's Ueshiba much more than that of any of the other karate masters. They say that Egami got a chance to watch Ueshiba demonstrate his techniques and that Ueshiba impressed Egami so much that he started to practice his karate in a more relaxed way. This may be the main reason he assumed this *kamae* for his book.

The photo to the right is of another Shotokai mas-

ter, Mitsusuke Harada (原田満祐, 1928–2021). He was the president of the Karate-do Shotokai (空手道 松濤會 [KDS]) and resided in the UK. He was known to teach his karate with ki. Therefore, even though his stance is close to *zenkutsu dachi* or *fudo dachi* (不動立ち), he has his hands open. The positions of his hands in this *kamae* is similar to that of Egami.

OK, let's look at two masters of Shotokan. The photo to the left shows a *kumite* scene between Hirokazu Kanazawa (金澤弘和, 1931–2019) on the left and Tetsuhiko Asai on the right. Both of them are assuming *zenkutsu dachi*. Kanazawa's style is a very standard Shotokan *kamae*

as his hands are held in *seiken*. Asai, on the other hand, is holding both of his hands open. Regardless, they represent pretty much the standard karate *kamae*.

The same thing can be said of the photo to the right, which is of Taiji Kase (加瀬泰治, 1929–2004), a well-known JKA instructor who lived and taught in France. His stance is *fudo dachi*, and he has his fists up like a street fighter or

boxer.

The photo to the left shows Asai facing Yoshiharu Osaka (大坂可治, 1947–). Against Kanazawa, he had his hands up. In this case, he was not particularly trying to strike or punch but to deliver different techniques with his arms. You can see that his hands are held totally down. This shows he had total control of the *kumite* situation.

This reminded me of the fighting style of Ali in some cases. When Ali felt he had total control, he kept his fists down as shown in the photo to the right. You can see that his opponent is keeping his fists near his face, fearing that Ali could strike him at any time, even when his fists are down. This is, in fact,

very interesting, at least to me. Most people would consider Ali to just be cocky or simply a show-off. That observation may be partially correct, but I believe he knew that having his fists low could also make him more effective. His attacking ability would, in fact, become more effective as his arm movements would become more unpredictable compared to the posture held by his opponent in the photo.

On the same token, I consider standing in *shizentai* (photo below left) to be more advantageous than the typical fighting stance similar to *zenkutsu dachi* that you find in *jiyu ippon kumite* or *jiyu kumite* (photo below right). I suspect many people will object and be opposed to my idea. You will probably tell me that the *kamae* used in *jiyu ippon kumite* or *jiyu kumite* is more effective or advantageous. I could agree if we were only discussing tournament or dojo *kumite* situations. But, in a real fight, that *kamae* with one foot forward could work against you. Let me explain.

First of all, by assuming that *kamae*, you are clearly expressing your intent to fight. This action may intimidate the opponent. It would be wonderful if your opponent got discouraged and decided not to fight. I wish this were the scenario every time. However, many a time, it may instigate or encourage him to fight, even if that was not his intention.

On the other hand, if your hands are down, then you do not look as though you wished to engage in a fight, and you do not look intimidating. When I say that your hands are down, this can include having them on your hips or lightly clasping them in front of you. Some people may want to include the arms-crossed position, but I do not include this arm position as this posture could convey an attitude of resistance or disagreement, which you most likely wish to avoid.

Secondly, as I mentioned earlier in the example of Ali's keeping his fists low, having your hands lower will give you more options as far as how you can use them. Yes, it is true that your hands are far away from your head, which is a very important area to protect. On the other hand, your hands are near the groin area, which is another critical target.

When you compare these two areas, it is far easier to dodge a strike, punch, or even a kick to the head by swaying or even ducking down. Even though kicking to the groin is not a very popular attacking technique in a street fight, it is much more difficult to dodge with just the movement of your hips alone. If your hands are near the groin area, you can either cover the critical area or block the kick using both hands.

The same thing can be said of a punch or strike to the midsection. You can block it easily with your dangling arm and a rotation of your upper body. A

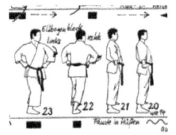

similar technique can be found in Steps 21–23 of Gankaku (岩鶴), where you hold your fists on your hips and rotate your hips to block with the right elbow first and then quickly follow that with the same block with the left elbow. You can do this technique even if you keep your arms straight down and achieve the same effect.

Finally, we have to pay attention to the position of the feet. Each one of us has a favorite side in his fighting style. Most people are right handed, so often-times they have their left foot forward. In this way, they can step in with the right foot to punch, or they can kick with the right foot. They can even keep the left foot forward in order to execute a right *gyaku zuki*. So, isn't this more advantageous? Once again, it may be in tournament or dojo *kumite*. But, in a street fight, you may have more than one opponent. If you commit your stance to, say, left foot forward, and a second opponent happens to be on your left side, he will be standing on your blind side. I am sure you do not wish to be in this situation. In addition, if your opponent happens to have a knife, stick, etc., you may want to have the option to turn around and run away. You can do this more easily if you are standing in *shizentai*.

Conclusion

I believe the best stance is shown by Musashi Miyamoto, whom I admire as I believe he was one of the best swordsman in history. Take a look at his very famous self-portrait (illustration right). Of course, we do not know for sure if he drew this to show the best *kamae*. However, this was drawn when he was fifty-six years old (1640), which was five years before his death. I assume he wanted to share with us what the best posture of a *kenjutsuka* would be.

Look how he stands. He assumes *shizentai* and holds both hands low. It is just like our *shizentai yoi* position (as Asai demonstrates in the photo to the left). In Miyamoto's portrait, he is holding a sword in each of his hands. I must assume that this is the fighting style Miyamoto considered to be the best. Look at his arms. They are held totally relaxed. He is not holding the swords like the kendo practitioners or the Jigen Ryu swordsman we saw earlier in the chapter.

I assume Miyamoto was confident that this was the most advantageous posture he could assume when facing an opponent. I concur with his belief, and, even for the empty-handed combat method of karate, when you engage in a real fight (not a tournament match), I consider the best stance to be one in which you stand in *shizentai* and hold your arms down naturally in *yoi* (用意) position.

I want to share one more photo of a karate master whom I respected deeply. His name was Seikichi Uehara (上原清吉1904–2004), the twelfth *soke* (宗家) of Motobu Ryu (本部流). He was unique not only because he lived to be a hundred years old but also because he was very active in karate training into his late nineties. Though he lived to be a hundred, he passed away about eighteen years ago.

He was an unparalleled expert and was also a little funny, though I am sure he did not intend to be. He wore a pair of suspenders and a cowboy hat as you can see in the photo to the right. Sometimes he wore a karate uniform, but he very frequently trained in street clothes. He also believed that a true *karateka* should be able to perform karate techniques while he was simply walking and demonstrated this in the video this photo was taken from. He said to never stop walking until all the fights were over. In the video I mentioned, he fights against about a dozen attackers. As they all successively attack him, he continues walking and defending himself against all of them in a very natural way.

Once again, I conclude that the best stance before the fight is *shizentai* with a *yoi* position. Once the fight starts, you must continue walking and moving until all the fights are finished. Considering this conclusion, it certainly makes good sense that in Asai Ryu karate, we emphasize very strongly the importance of *kihon ippon kumite* (基本一本組手, 'basic single-attack sparring'). In fact, we place more emphasis on this drill than on *jiyu ippon kumite* or *jiyu kumite*.

CHAPTER THIRTEEN
第十三章

WHAT IS SEN IN KENJUTSU?
剣術での先とは何か

In kenjutsu, *sen* is a very important fighting concept. In fact, there are three kinds of *sen*. They are *go no sen*, *sen no sen*, and *sensen no sen*.

These three concepts are very important and well known not only in kenjutsu and kendo but also in other martial arts. However, they are not well known among karate practitioners. In fact, there are a few reasons they are not practiced or studied among *karateka*. In this chapter, I will explain what these three concepts mean. And, at the end, I will share my thoughts on why they are not well practiced or studied much among karate practitioners.

First, let's look at the character used to write *sen*: 先. If you are adept at recognizing kanji or are a senior practitioner, you may notice that this character is part of the familiar terms *sensei* (先生) and *senpai* (先輩). Of course, you already know the meaning of these terms. Interestingly, the literal meanings of these two terms are not 'instructor' and 'senior student'. For instance, *sensei* simply refers to a person who was born earlier.

In fact, the character for *sen* is very interesting and also mysterious. It can be sort of confusing because it can refer to both the past and the future. Don't you agree that this is strange? I will explain a little later why this is the case.

In addition, you need to know that the character 先 can be read in two different ways. One reading is *sen* (as used in *sensei*). The other reading is *saki*. Since our discussion is not about the Japanese language, I will not go into why a character can have two or more different readings. Depending on the context (not on the reading), this character can mean one thing or another. I suspect this can be very confusing to many readers.

Here are some examples of terms that have a meaning related to the past:

- *Sensei* (先生, 'teacher' [lit., 'born earlier'])
- *Senjitsu* (先日, 'the other day')
- *Senshu* (先週, 'last week')

- *Sensenshu* (先々週, 'the week before last')
- *Senzo* (先祖, 'ancestor')
- *Senjin* (先人, 'predecessor')

As you can see from the examples listed above, when we read 先 as *sen*, it typically refers to the past. However, there are other terms using the *sen* reading that mean 'front' or 'ahead'.

- *Sentan* (先端, 'front side', 'front edge')
- *Sento* (先頭, 'front [of a line]')

If it is read as *saki*, it usually means 'front' or 'ahead'. Here are some examples:

- *Kore kara saki* (これから先, 'ahead of us', 'from now on')
- *Ichinen saki* (一年先, 'a year from now')
- *Kensaki* (剣先, 'point of a sword')

Once again, it can also mean the opposite and refer to the past. Here are a few examples of the past usage:

- *Saki no shusho* (先の首相, 'former prime minister')
- *Saki no taisen* (先の大戦, 'the last world war')
- *Saki no shujin* (先の主人, 'late husband', 'ex-husband')

Now that you are totally confused, I must explain why this character is this way.

Sen essentially refers to something that is ahead of a position in relation to the direction of a line or progression. This is why *sentan* indicates the front side or front edge and *sento* refers to the front of a line. Now you understand that *sen* refers to the front when you think of a location or a line. This is the main concept you must understand.

However, the same character can refer to something in the past, such as *senpai*, which is a student who joined a particular dojo or organization at an earlier time. How can this refer to the past? It is because a *senpai* is positioned earlier in time/seniority.

In the Western world, a *senpai* is understood to be a student of a higher rank. However, ranks are not considered in this term. Even though a *senpai* tends to be of a higher rank, his higher rank does not necessarily make him a *senpai*. In Japan, the role of *senpai* is determined only by the date the person joined the dojo. If you joined your dojo earlier than another person, then, regardless of current or future rank, you will continue to be *senpai* to any student who joined later.

How do we explain *sensei* as being a teacher or instructor? This is much easier to understand. A person who was born earlier than the students is expected to have learned more and know more. For this reason, he can teach the students, who are younger and supposedly know less.

"Teacher"

se n   se i
せん   せい
先生
"Previous"   "Life"

You may feel that I have given you more than enough explanation for the word *sen*. However, understanding this particular Japanese word is necessary for understanding the deep concept of *sen* used in the martial art of kenjutsu.

Now we can say we are ready to move on to the *budo* sense of *sen*. As I explained earlier, *sen*, in the *budo* sense, means 'ahead' or 'earlier'. But, we must think in the sense of not only time but also timing and tempo. These senses seem to be similar but are quite different. We will discuss this further and take a look at more details as we get into the explanation of each of the three different *sen* concepts.

Let us start with the concept of *go no sen*. This one is probably the most well known and also the most favored in karate. Toward the end of this chapter, we will discuss the reasons *go no sen* is favored among karate practitioners.

Go no Sen (後の先)

The character *go* (後) means 'after', 'late', 'back', or 'afterward'. The word *no* (の) between the two kanji is equivalent to the preposition *of* in English (but used in reverse order). Therefore, *go no sen* refers to the concept of enticing the opponent to initiate his attack in order to cause him to make a mistake that can then be exploited. I suspect some readers will ask for further explanation in order to better understand the concept. Of course, senior practitioners may already understand this concept fully.

For those who are not sure of this concept, here is an explanation using some examples. When you think of *kihon kumite*, such as *ippon kumite* and *jiyu ippon kumite*, you can see this concept clearly. In these *kumite* situations, the opponent announces what attack he will execute, such as *jodan*,

chudan, *mae geri* (前蹴り), etc. The key point in *go no sen* is that you let or make the opponent attack first. In other words, you sort of wait until the opponent makes the initial move (usually an attack).

A typical *go no sen* strategy in *kumite* is to open (meaning not using your arms and/or stance to assume a defensive *kamae*) an area (usually *chudan* more often than *jodan*) and entice the opponent to attack that area. For instance, a good kicker (competitor K) may be enticed to throw a *mae geri* if the *go no sen* practitioner (competitor G) purposely opens the *chudan* section by dropping his arms down or spreading them wide. When K kicks G as expected, G will use his hand to receive the kick with *sukui uke* (掬い受け, 'scooping block') and throw

K off-balance while simultaneously countering with *gyaku zuki* to score a point. It is also a popular strategy to induce the opponent to initiate a certain attacking technique, such as *gyaku zuki, mae geri, oi zuki*, etc.

By knowing ahead of time exactly what attack is coming, you can easily block or dodge and execute an effective counterattack. The opponent's attack will miss the target and be rendered ineffective. Your counter, on the other hand, is effective and brings you victory in the fight. Your attack is, indeed, after or later than (*go*) the opponent's attack. However, by controlling the situation and nullifying the opponent's attack, you capture the first or earlier (*sen*) opportunity to defeat the opponent.

Even though *go no sen* is the most favored in karate, interestingly, it is the least recommended in kenjutsu and kendo.

Sen no Sen (先の先)

This concept is sometimes referred to simply as *sen* (先) or *tsui no sen* (対の 先).

There are two *sen* in this term. This means that your first attack is ahead of your opponent's first attack. In other words, this is a situation where you see your opponent move to attack, so you attack him before he can complete his attack.

Let me illustrate this concept using the following imaginary situation. Your opponent finds an opportunity to attack, and you detect his initial move. You and your opponent execute your attacking techniques almost simultaneously. Since you saw the opponent's initial move and were better prepared, you can land your technique before your opponent can. From the outside, it may look as though both parties moved at the same time. This is why this concept's other name is *tsui no sen*. The character 対 means 'pair' or 'couple'.

At many *kumite* tournaments, I have seen where competitors immediately attack each other as soon as the judge says, "*Hajime!*" They may want to consider this to be *sen no sen*. Unfortunately, most of them have little strategy and tactics.

They just jump in and see if they can score a point. I do not consider this technique to be *sen no sen*. A good competitor should be able to induce or force the opponent to move when he is not really ready by using various tactics, including distances, openings, and feints.

An excellent example of *sen no sen* can be viewed in the movie *Seven Samurai*. I referenced this film earlier, and many senior practitioners might have seen it as it became a big hit right after it was produced and continued to be one of the most favored samurai movies in the sixties and seventies.

One of the seven samurai is challenged by an overconfident samurai. The challenge is accepted, and the two of them fight with *bokken* (木剣, 'wooden swords') to see who is faster. After a tense moment, they swing their swords down, seemingly at the same time. Since it is an informal *shiai* (試合, 'match', 'tournament'), they do not hit each other. Both of them stop their swords right before they hit the target. The guy who issued the challenge says it is a draw, but the guy who accepted the challenge says he is faster.

If you have already seen this movie, you know what happens next. They decide to fight again, but this time they use real swords to settle the disagreement. The samurai who was challenged proves he is right. Even though they seem to swing their swords down at the same time, the samurai who was challenged is faster, and the challenger has to learn by losing his life. Here is the scene in question: www.youtube.com/watch?v=GF5U83UIX1o.

Sensen no Sen (先先の先)

I assume the first two ideas were not so difficult. What is challenging to understand clearly is *sensen no sen*. It is somewhat confusing, even to Japanese people, as this term has three instances of the same *sen* character. *Sensen no sen* means that your first attack comes ahead of your opponent's first attack. On the surface, *sen no sen* and *sensen no sen* may look similar, if not the same, even when viewed by Japanese martial artists.

Some say that in *sensen no sen*, you have the ability to detect the opponent's brain waves when he decides to move or attack. In other words, there is a split-second delay (as short as 0.3 seconds) between his wish to move (the impulse in his brain) and his actual physical move. If you can detect this brain impulse, then you can "read" whatever he plans to do. It is as if you had radar ability. It is a historical fact that England was able to defeat the German air force mainly because of this equipment they developed in the early 1940s. This ability to know in advance is, of course, very desirable. However, it is also extremely difficult for a martial artist to acquire and develop.

OK, I have provided a summary of the three *sen* concepts. Let's look at what Musashi Miyamoto said about this subject. In the *Hi no Maki* (火の巻, 'Volume of Fire') of his book *Gorin no Sho* (五輪書, 'The Book of Five Rings'), Miyamoto says that there are three kinds of *sen*. I will quote what he wrote in Japanese and then provide two different translations of his statement below.

三つの先、一つは我が方より敵へかかる先、「懸の先」と云也。亦一つは、敵より我の方にかかる時の先、是は、「待の先」と云也。又一つは、我もかかり、敵もかかりあふ時の先、「体々の先」と云。是三つの先也。いづれの戦初めにも、此三つの先より外はなし。先の次第を以て、はや勝事を得る物なれば、先と云事兵法の第一也。

This first translation is from Philosophical Investigations for Applied Linguistics.

There are three types in preemptive moves. One is a preemptive move from me to the opponent, and it is called the *active preemptive move*. Another is a preemptive move when the opponent is to strike me, and it is called the *reactive preemptive move*. The last is a preemptive move when both the opponent and I are to strike each other, and it is called the *interactive preemptive move*. There is no other type in preemptive moves. As a preemptive move is the decisive factor in victory, it is the most crucial in martial arts. There are many details in a preemptive move, but as it is up to the Logos of the moment and you need to see the mind of the opponent and use the wisdom of martial arts to win, I just cannot specify a preemptive move. (yosukeyanase. blogspot.com/2012/03/comparing-foreign-language.html)

What Miyamoto is saying is very complex, and I would like to add my translation below. I hope it will help you better understand his statement.

There are three *sen*. One is to attack the opponent before he gets ready. This one is called *ken no sen*. Another is to attack after the opponent attacks you first. This one is called *tai no sen*. The last one is called *taitai no sen*. This is the situation where you attack as soon as the opponent attacks you. These three cases are the three *sen*. Each one is fighting timing, but there is no timing other than these three. By mastering the proper *sen*, you can always achieve victory; thus, *sen* is the most important concept in the martial arts.

To assist you in understanding what he is saying, let me add a couple of my opinions here. What he calls *ken no sen*, I consider to be the same as *sensen no sen*. Similarly, his *tai no sen* must be what we call *go no sen*.

If you practice kendo, you know that there are some kendo *kata*. In fact, there are a total of ten: seven that use the long sword and three that use the short sword. Performing *kata* is required for *dan* examinations. This must mean *kata* is important in kendo, which is very interesting.

Let me explain the structure of kendo *kata*. The *shitachi* (仕太刀) is the defender and always waits for the *uchitachi* (打太刀) to attack first. In every *kata* match, the *shitachi* wins, and *uchitachi* loses in the end.

This is not a surprise for karate practitioners. Our *kihon kumite* is designed the same way. The attacker always initiates the fight, and the defender blocks the attack and counterattacks. There are some variations in *kihon kumite* where the attacker blocks the defender's counter and ends up being the winner. However, in most cases, the defender is the winner in *kihon kumite*. This basic design is not a surprise if you realize that the idea of *kihon kumite* came from kendo in the early twentieth century.

It seems to me that this design of *kata* and *kumite* only makes it possible to learn *go no sen* (where the defender blocks the opponent's attack and then counters) and *sen no sen* (where both sides attack almost at the same time but the defender wins in the end). This naturally makes me wonder how kendo and karate practitioners can learn *sensen no sen*. I will cover this important point at the end of this chapter.

One famous kendo master from the last century, Sasaburo Takano (高野佐三郎, 1862–1950), said that there are two kinds of *sen*. One is action, and the other is ki or mind. What he was saying was that if you can read the opponent's ki or mind and predict all of his actions, then your later action can be understood as the result of *sensen no sen*. Does this make sense to you?

By practicing the set movements of *kata*, the defender will learn to catch or feel the opponent's ki before he moves. Initially, meaning while you are still at the lower *dan* levels, you move as you see the opponent's movement. This is a reactionary movement, and you will never be able to act before the opponent. You may achieve it occasionally but only by guessing the timing.

This feeling out of the opponent's ki can be seen in the Japanese movie I mentioned earlier, *Seven Samurai*. I already referenced this scene briefly back in Chapter 3, but I will give a more detailed explanation here. The characters are selecting an expert from among the passing samurai. They invite several candidates to go into the house for an interview. One of the samurai hides behind the

door with a wooden sword held above his
head and waits for each candidate to walk
through. If the candidate fails to detect the
danger, he is hit in the head. Many candidates fail; however, one candidate stops in
front of the entrance and yells to the waiting
samurai, "You must be joking!" Of course,

this candidate passes the test and is invited to join the group.

Once you learn to read or feel the opponent's ki, you have total control. In
other words, you can strike anytime you wish, either before or after the opponent's first move. This is why *sensen no sen* is considered to be the most important or sought-after *sen* in kendo.

Interestingly, *go no sen* is considered to be the least important. In fact, in
many cases, especially if you wait idly for the opponent's attack, it is called *ma-
chiken* (待ち剣, 'waiting sword'). This tactic is very much discouraged in kendo.
Practitioners are instructed not to wait but rather to entice or force the opponent
to attack, which is called *go no sen*.

Master Takano said there was only *seme* (攻め, 'attack') in kendo. The
concept of *uke* must not be considered to be a separate entity from that of *seme*.
Rather, it must be included in the concept of *seme*. In other words, the block must
be executed as part of the attack. This concept is often misunderstood to mean
that the block is executed so hard or so strongly that it repels the attack. There
may be such a block used in a fight. However, the concept Takano was referring
to does not necessarily mean that the block must be hard or strong.

Now that we understand the basic concepts of the three different types of
sen, let's go back and discuss why *go no sen* is the most favored among karate
practitioners.

As we saw in *sensen no sen*, if you can predict all of the opponent's moves
before he makes them, you have the option to hit him before he moves. You
could also purposely let the opponent make his move first. If you predict what

he is going to do, you can easily block or dodge and then strike him. The latter option would look like *go no sen*, but it is slightly different and is *sensen no sen*. If *karateka* understood this and favored *go no sen* for this reason, I would be very happy. However, I suspect most *karateka* favor *go no sen* for different reasons.

I want to share two major reasons for this trend. One is Master Funakoshi's famous concept of *Karate ni sente nashi* (which I mentioned in

Chapter 9). Because of this, the concept that karate starts and ends with an *uke* became widely used. Even though I think Funakoshi meant that a *karateka* must not instigate a fight rather than referring to an actual fighting strategy, I am afraid his true intention has been misunderstood by many followers. What is interesting is that this concept is shared even among Okinawan practitioners. The reason for this, I think, resides in the second fact of modern-day karate.

I mentioned this briefly in Chapter 9, but many readers may not know that the practice of any martial art was prohibited throughout Japan after World War II. Of course, karate was one of the prohibited activities. The karate masters approached GHQ and tried to convince those in charge that karate was not an aggressive art. They claimed that it was a weaponless art (though this was not true) and a purely defensive art. Many of the karate masters on Okinawa joined this movement because many American GIs stationed on Okinawa had shown strong interest in learning the art of karate.

Believe it or not, karate was the first martial art to receive permission from GHQ to be practiced in Japan. It started being taught in 1946 (a year after the war had ended), whereas kendo had to wait for permission until 1952. To prove

that karate was a defensive art, the instructors at that time had to tell their students that karate starts and ends with an *uke*. I suspect many of them believed in adopting the other concept of *Sente hissho* (also mentioned in Chapter 9) in an actual fight. But, after more than seventy years since that time, the average karate instructor believes this was the genuine philosophy of ancient karate. Thus, it is believed that it must be maintained.

Conclusion

So, the conclusion is that *sensen no sen* is the most desired in kenjutsu and that *go no sen* based on *sensen no sen* is the most favored in karate. Though we understand this, the challenging question is how we can develop such an ability. In other words, how can we read the opponent's mind? Even if we agree that such a thing is possible, we are not taught how to develop this ability beyond just being told that we must practice more.

I do not believe that just training more will naturally result in this ability. In fact, an irresponsible and incapable instructor would say this to avoid confessing that he does not know how to develop it.

I am one of those incapable instructors who do not know how to read the brain waves of the opponent. However, I may be able to provide a few hints here. I do not claim that these hints will help the reader, but they are at least helping my training. One day I may be able to catch all of my opponent's brain waves so that I can achieve *sensen no sen*.

I believe this ability requires mental training more than physical. In other words, instead of engaging in more *kumite* practice, you should spend more time in meditation and calming your mind. Brain waves can be detected and measured via medical methods such as electroencephalography (EEG). However, they are very minute, and most of us do not feel or detect them. Therefore, to detect such minute brain waves, you must have an extremely calm and sensible mind. It is obvious that when your mind is turbulent or messy, your mental ability is low, and you cannot detect minute changes in the brain waves coming from another person. This is why I recommend meditation to sharpen your mind.

In fact, this is exactly what the ancient samurai did to improve their swordsmanship. Of course they practiced their fencing in the dojo, but they realized they needed more. They realized that they needed to calm their mind in order to achieve *sensen no sen*. Thus, they chose to meditate either at Zen Buddhist temples or under waterfalls.

The other method is to pay more attention to your heart. In 1991, a medical team headed by Dr. J. Andrew Armour found that our heart has 40,000 of its own neurons that are unique and independent. The heart, amazingly, can "think," "remember," and "dictate" actions in a way that is similar to that of the brain. Some medical doctors say the heart is a small brain comparable to the main brain inside the head. This is not speculation or hypothesis. It is a medical fact. I believe the heart is what we call the *chutanden* (中丹田, 'middle *tanden*'), the source of ki.

As far as I know, this statement has never been expressed by anyone. In other words, up until now, the experts have not equated the *chutanden* to the heart. We typically believe that the heart is a physical part that pumps blood in and out and that that's all it does. But, a recent medical discovery has proven this belief wrong. The heart is more than that.

For those who are skeptical, read the medical article "The Little 'Brain in the Heart,'" which can be found here: www.heartmath.org/our-heart-brain/. That same article also recommends the e-book *Science of the Heart*, which can be downloaded here: www.heartmath.org/research/science-of-the-heart/. It is good investment of your time if you are serious about learning what the heart can do in human performance.

The fact that the heart has a memory function has been proven in the cases of many heart-transplant patients. After their operations, some found new habits, likes, and dislikes. Through investigation, they discovered that those new tendencies had

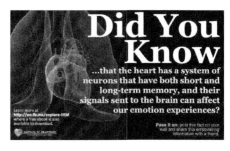

been exhibited by the organ donors, as well. If you do not believe this, you can check medical studies on this subject, and you will find documented cases.

So, why am I writing about this newfound ability of the heart? I am proposing that if we can coordinate the ability of the heart with that of the brain, the combination of the abilities of these two brains can increase our overall mental ability, including the detection of brain waves or ki.

I do not think this is a ridiculous or inconsequential idea given that we agree that women have a keener sense than men. They have a keener ability to feel or detect the gaze of others. I think females have this ability not only because they tend to be victims of physical attacks but also because they know (albeit unconsciously) how to use their heart (or feelings) along with their mind (brain) to cope with the environment and people around them, whereas men tend to depend solely on their brain to make judgments or deal with situations, resulting in poorer outcomes.

My recommendations are meditation and more attention to your heart to improve your ability to read your opponent's mind. Even if you are not able to achieve such an ability, I guarantee that you will have a more peaceful mind and will be happier. Isn't this one of the objectives of karate training?

CHAPTER FOURTEEN
第十四章

THE MYSTERY OF KNEE JOINTS
膝関節の不思議

Believe it or not, the knee joint is a very interesting part of the body. It is interesting as it is not only very important but also very delicate and can be fragile.

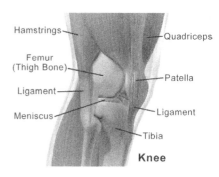

According to the National Center for Biotechnology Information (NCBI), the knee is the joint that is most commonly injured by adolescent athletes. An estimated 2.5 million sports-related injuries present to emergency departments each year. The NCBI also states that 6.6 million knee injuries were reported to United States emergency departments from 1999 through 2008. Here is the relevant article: www.ncbi.nlm.nih.gov/pubmed/22506941.

National Center for Biotechnology Information

Obviously, we know the knee joint is important as we cannot even stand up, let alone walk or run, if we have any problems with our knees. So, why is it so delicate and possibly fragile? According to the Smithsonian National Museum of Natural History, approximately 300,000 years ago, Homo sapiens evolved in Africa. Ever since then, we have been walking on two legs. So, why do we often have problems with our knee joints?

I am not a medical expert or an anthropologist or an expert in osteology. I am simply sharing my own thoughts and my hypothesis. If you believe in the theory of evolution, we evolved from apes. The ancestors of the apes were four-legged mammals (dogs, cats, cows, horses, etc.). When our ancestors (pre-Homo sapiens) stood up on their two hind legs, the angle of the joint, as well as the pressure point of the body weight, shifted dramatically. The

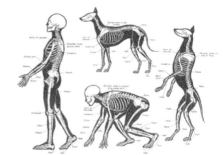

burden was doubled when our body started to be supported by only two legs. In addition, standing on two legs requires a fine balancing act. They say that our body, though invisible to us, is always swaying in different directions in order for us to keep our balance while we are standing up.

Now back to the injury subject. Again, according to the NCBI, an estimated 6.6 million knee injuries occurred in a period of nine years. This is an amazing rate of more than two knee injuries per thousand people. I am pretty sure the reader will agree that these figures are quite high. In other words, knee injuries

are very common. These numbers are for the general population, so the number of injuries would most likely go up significantly for a group who engages in athletics, dances, or participates in other physical activities, including karate.

Here is an excellent article entitled "Knee Pain in Martial Arts: Causes and Remedies," which can be found on the website for Full Potential Martial Arts Academy in Carmel Valley, California, U.S.A.: www.fullpotentialma.com/knee-pain-in-martial-arts-causes-and-remedies/.

The reason I decided to write this chapter was that I posted a short video entitled "Georgian National Ballet" on my Facebook page. That video showed the Sukhishvili Georgian National Ballet team's dance rehearsal and can be found here: www.youtube.com/watch?v=apnNtpo81_g.

I was very impressed with the dance that was performed by the young men in Georgia. It involved not only many spins and turns but also several quick kneeling and jumping actions. When I posted the video, I wrote, "This proves that if you train diligently and correctly, these kinds of moves will not result in knee problems."

One reader who happens to be my

karate colleague and whom I respect very much wrote back, saying that not all knees were the same. His point was that not everyone can dance as well as these dancers because people's knees are different.

I pushed back respectfully with the statement that I believed knees were created the same in general among all the races and in both men and women. I added, "The difference is how you train your ligaments and the muscles in the legs, particularly around the knees. Anyone, provided they train correctly, can do what these dancers are doing. These skills can be adopted in the martial arts, as well."

To this comment, another karate colleague whom I also respect very much provided me with an article written for USC News by Jennifer Chan. The title of the article is "All Knees Are Not Created Equal," and it can be found here: news. usc.edu/19138/All-Knees-Are-Not-Created-Equal.

USC News is produced and edited by USC University Communications. Articles are written by University Communications staff and writers from USC schools and administrative units. This article was written by the University Communications staff, so it must be reliable. The title was opposed to what I had stated but was interesting, so I read it. Here are some quotes from the article:

- Each year, nearly half a million Americans receive knee replacements to relieve pain and disability.
- According to a recent survey, two-thirds of the primary recipients are women because they tend to live longer than men, thereby incurring more joint wear.
- Surgeons have realized that the unique differences between the female and male anatomy of the knee were not being addressed with traditional knee replacement options.

- The size and shape of the female knee bones, including the femur, tibia and patella, are significantly different from men.
- Female knees are thinner and have a slight difference in angle between the femur and tibia than male knees, so the gender-specific knee ensures precise articulation that allows for a more natural movement.

The rest of the article talked about how they had developed knee replacements specific to the needs of each gender, which assures better and more successful knee-replacement surgeries.

What I concluded from this article is that, despite the fact that there is a difference between the knee joints of each sex, this is mainly a difference in size. There are more women who get knee replacements, but they concluded that this is mainly because women live longer than men. It is natural to see more joint problems as they become very old. Therefore, I did not see any message in this article that indicated that the difference between the knee joints of each sex would make either sex inferior or show that one had a higher tendency to have knee problems.

Despite this conclusion, I decided to further investigate the differences between the structures of the knee joints of each sex. So, I came across an excerpt from the book *Women's Strength Training Anatomy* (Human Kinetics, 2002). The author, Frédéric Delavier, studied morphology and anatomy for five years at the prestigious École des Beaux-Arts in Paris and studied dissection for three years at the Paris Faculté de Médecine.

The excerpt is on the skeletal differences between women and men. This is only one page, and I believe the information is beneficial to the reader, so I will quote the entire excerpt here:

The morphological differences between women and men are the result of differences in the volume and proportion of similar anatomical features. Generally speaking, the female skeleton is not as massive; it is smoother and more delicate with impressions—hollows or bumps—that serve as muscle insertions or provide passage for tendons, which are less accentuated. (The more highly developed musculature in men marks the skeleton more.) The female thoracic cage is generally more rounded

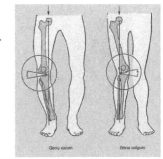

and not as big as in the male. Proportionately, the skeletal width of the shoulders is the same as in the male, but the larger muscular development of the latter makes it seem wider. The lumbar curve is greater in women and the pelvis is tilted anteriorly (anteversion), which makes for the sway-backed appearance often found in women. If the waist in women is longer and smaller, it is because the thorax is more constricted at the base and the pelvis is generally not as high.

The most important difference between the male and female skeletons is found at the level of the pelvis. The female pelvis is adapted for gestation: it is not as high and is proportionately wider than that of the male. The sacrum of the female is wider and the pelvic ring is wider and more circular to facilitate the passage of the newborn. As the pelvic ring is wider, the acetabula (the fossa in which the heads of the femurs lodge) are farther apart, which increases the distance between the greater trochanters and consequently the width of the hips.

Greater hip width in women influences the position of the femurs, which are often more angled than in men, giving them a slight X shape.

A wide pelvis with a significant angle of the femur can provoke genu valgum, accentuated all the more by the hyperlaxity toward which women tend. The legs then take on a typical X shape: the articulation at the knee is excessively solicited; the medial collateral ligament is overstretched; and the lateral meniscus, the cartilage-covered articular surfaces of the external condyle of the femur, and the lateral tuberosity of the tibia are subjected to excessive loads, which may lead to premature wear.

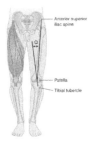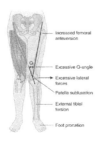

Pathological genu valgum is accompanied by medial collapse at the ankle and the disappearance of the plantar arch (flat foot), which may involve pain because of excessive stretching of certain muscles in the sole of the foot.

It is very important to take into account the individual morphologies and to remember that women are more often prone to genu valgum pathologies, whereas men more frequently suffer from bow-legs (genu varum). People with very noticeable genu valgum should therefore work out carefully, avoid training with heavy weights, and always perform the movements so as to avoid impacts that would aggravate knee and ankle problems. (us.humankinetics.com/blogs/excerpt/see-the-skeletal-differences-between-women-and-men#:~:text=This%20is%20an%20excerpt%20from,proportion%20 of%20similar%20anatomical%20features)

What I took away from this article is as follows:

1. Generally speaking, the female skeleton is not as massive.
2. The most important difference between the male and female skeletons is found at the level of the pelvis.
3. The wide pelvis and significant angle of the femur in women can provoke genu valgum, or being knock-kneed.
4. Men, on the other hand, more frequently suffer from genu varum, or being bowlegged.

I agree fully that the skeletal structure of a man is different from that of a woman. However, it does not mean that either sex has inferior bone structure, which includes the knee joint. Women tend to have a knock-knee problem, but, at the same time, men tend to have a bowleg problem.

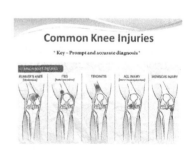

Thus, both sexes can develop some kind of knee problem or injury either by accident or with age.

Before I arrived at my final conclusion, I wanted to check one more article written by an orthopedic specialist. I found such an article written by Dr. Brett Greenky and Dr. Seth Greenky.

Dr. Brett Greenky is an orthopedic surgeon specializing in knee and joint replacement. He has been an active surgeon and lecturer in the field of joint arthroplasty for twenty-three years. As associate professor in orthopedics at Upstate Medical University, he has trained over 105 surgeons in the art of joint arthroplasty while codirecting the joint-replacement program at St. Joseph's Hospital in Syracuse.

Dr. Greenky has implanted more than 7500 joint implants over the last twenty-three years and currently offers nearly 500 new patients implants each year. The joint-replacement program at the Center for Orthopedic & Spine Care at St. Joseph's Hospital, which he codirects, is the most active program in Central New York.

Dr. Seth Greenky is a reconstructive orthopedic surgery specialist in Fayetteville, New York, U.S.A., and has over thirty-nine years of experience in the medical field. He graduated from SUNY Upstate Medical University (Syracuse) in 1983. He is affiliated with medical facilities such as Crouse Hospital and St. Joseph's Hospital Health Center. He currently practices at Syracuse Orthopedic Specialists and is board certified in orthopedic surgery.

These two wrote an article in 2015 entitled "Gender Differences in Joint Replacement," in which they state the following:

> Joint replacement surgery is increasingly common in the United States. Converging social and medical realities are making the incidence of degenerative joint disease of the weight-bearing joints (hip and knee) increasingly prevalent. It is estimated that more than 1 million knee replacements and nearly 600,000 hip replacements will be done yearly by 2020.

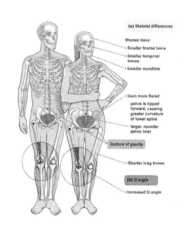

They go on to cover the gender differences:

> Women more commonly need total knee replacement compared to men. The need for hip replacement is about even between the sexes. Age-matched men versus women: men put slightly more miles per year on their joints. Men average a million steps

per year at age 65, while women average about 800,000 steps during the same time frame. The number of steps per year goes down about 3% annually in both genders. Men weigh more, so the wear placed on the joints is certainly higher than women. Men tolerate metal-on-metal hip surfaces better than women, who seem to have a special sensitivity to these implants. Women have a higher incidence of inflammatory arthritis like rheumatism (actually nearly 9:1). (www.sosbones.com/news/gender-differences-in-joint-replacement/)

Once again, experienced surgeons state that men have more problems with their knee joints because they walk more than women in general. Another reason for the more frequent problems is body weight, men being generally heavier than women. There was no mention of the inferiority of the knee joint of either sex.

It is true that the knee joints of men and women are created differently. Osteology experts tell us that women's knees are generally smaller. Due to the difference in pelvis width, the angle of the femur in relation to the tibia is different for each sex. The extreme tilt, either inward or outward, could cause a potential knee-joint problem. However, the risk is the same, or very similar, for both sexes.

In addition, I have not discovered any medical or osteological research finding that there is any structural difference among the nationalities and races. In other words, the knee joint of a Japanese person is basically identical to that of an American, European, African, etc.

I do believe, however, that cultural differences, particularly those relating to lifestyle, can have an effect. For instance, your knees do not bend too much while sitting in a chair. Sitting in *seiza* (正座), on the other hand, which is something found in Japanese martial arts,  requires hyperflexion of the knees and much stretching of the knee ligaments. This way of sitting was very common and popular in the Japanese lifestyle but has been disappearing lately.

Many Western *karateka* falsely believe that the Japanese have a superior knee structure. Unfortunately, this is incorrect. Many Japanese children have a lifestyle of sitting only in chairs these days. They no longer sit on the floor. What do you think happens to them as a consequence? They cannot do bunny hops or sit in the *seiza* position. They now have as many knee-joint problems as Western children.

It is true that knee problems often occur due to extreme twisting of the leg, excessive impact to the joint, hyperextension, etc. Karate training involves lots of body shifting, turning, and kicking. This means practitioners should develop their physical ability to match the training requirements.

Practitioners must learn the correct stances and body-shifting methods. They also should warm up their joints before each training session. In addition, they must supplement their warm-ups with some specific exercises to strengthen the muscles and ligaments that hold

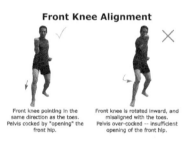

Front Knee Alignment

Front knee pointing in the same direction as the toes. Pelvis cocked by "opening" the front hip.

Front knee is rotated inward, and misaligned with the toes. Pelvis over-cocked -- insufficient opening of the front hip.

the knee joint. Practitioners must advance only gradually in their training and in the more challenging techniques. They must not engage in exercises and training that cause any pain to the joints. The sense of pain is an indication that something is wrong.

The dance performed by the Sukhishvili Georgian National Ballet team seems extreme and dangerous to an audience that has never trained for it. However, through muscle preparation and physical conditioning, anyone can learn to dance like those ballet dancers, even though not everyone can become good enough to be a member of their team.

On the same token, some of the Asai Ryu physical exercises, such as bunny hops, one-legged squats, jumps from *seiza*, etc., seem extreme, and even dangerous, to karate practitioners who have never trained for them. I request that the reader not dismiss these exercises or categorize them as being unhealthy or dangerous without giving them a fair trial.

Conclusion

I want to emphasize very strongly that almost anyone can become a karate expert without ruining his knees if he exercises well and trains correctly. I am seventy-five years old, and I can demonstrate any of these Asai exercises. I am not an exception or a superman. I have trained regularly and have trained under some excellent instructors. Thus, I have never experienced any joint injuries, including knee and hip injuries, in my life. In addition, I train three to four hours daily, even to this day, in order to maintain my condition and prepare myself for action. Training this much time may be too difficult for most practitioners. But, they can spend much less time and still avoid joint problems if they train in karate properly.

On the other hand, if you claim that you are an instructor or call yourself *Sensei*, then you are obligated to dedicate your time to making yourself worthy of the title. If you already have a knee- or hip-joint problem, the least you can do is to teach and train your students correctly so that they will not suffer from the same problem. I believe this is a universal obligation of a sensei. Am I asking too much? What do you think?

CHAPTER FIFTEEN
第十五章

WHAT IS SHINTAI O TSUNAGU?
身体を繋ぐとは？

The title of this chapter is "What Is Shintai o Tsunagu?" Of course, most readers do not speak Japanese, so this title is nothing but a mystery. So, let me explain what the Japanese words mean to start with. *Shintai* (身体) means 'body', and here it refers to the human body in particular. *O* (を) is grammatical particle that identifies the word before it as the object of the verb, so we need to know what the verb *tsunagu* (繋ぐ) means in order to see the relationship to the body. Well, the verb *tsunagu* means 'connect', 'tie', 'fasten', or 'link'.

Let's put these words together and see what they mean. The idea would be to connect, tie, fasten, or link the body. This most likely does not make too much sense to you. You may ask, "Connect or fasten the body to what?"

It may come as a surprise to the reader, but the connection is not to anything outside the body. In fact, the connecting, tying, fastening, or linking happens inside the body. This means we need to do some study on the physiology of the body. Believe it or not, it has a very complex and intricate construction. Since this is not for medical purposes, I will cover this topic only superficially and give a summary of the various key parts of the body. I hope this journey will be beneficial to all readers.

THE MUSCULAR SYSTEM

All of us are aware that we can move (e.g., stand, sit, walk, etc.) because we have bones and muscles. By the way, do you know how many muscles and bones we have in our body? Unless you are in the medical field, you most likely do not know the answer to this question. According to Jill Seladi-Schulman, PhD, "It's estimated that there are over 650 named skeletal muscles in your body." Did you guess that we had so many muscles? I bet you guessed fewer. If you are interested in learning more about muscles, here is the full article: www.healthline.com/health/how-many-muscles-are-in-the-human-body.

We know that the skeletal muscles are attached to the bones via tendons, and this is how we can move. When a muscle tenses or contracts, the attached bone

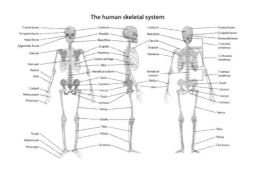

The human skeletal system

will move. OK, let's see how many bones we have in our body. According to the Bodytomy website (bodytomy.com/how-many-bones-are-in-human-body), "the adult human skeleton consists of 206 bones." Did you guess this? I bet your guess was different, but that is OK. That is not a problem as most of us are not familiar with these details.

On second thought, don't you agree that *karateka*, especially instructors, should have some knowledge of how our body is constructed? Unfortunately, many do not pay much attention to this important subject. Well, this is why I am writing this chapter. But, it is not important to know exactly how many bones and muscles we have. If you have a rough idea, that is sufficient. What is important is how they work.

You may move your arms and fingers and say, "Heck, it is easy. I know exactly how they work." I am sure you truly believe that you do. But, I respectfully disagree. Let me challenge you. What is one thing a muscle is unable to do? I will give you a few minutes to think about it.

Do you have the answer? Before we get to that, we know that a muscle can tense. If you bend your arm like Popeye, you find a small (or large) bulge on your upper arm. Yes, you tensed the biceps. As you can see in this illustration of the muscles of the arm, there is another group of muscles there, the triceps. In order for you to make a bulge with the biceps, what do you have to do with the triceps? Some may say, "Extend them." Others may say, "Relax them." But, which one is correct?

The Anatomy of the Arm (or The Brachium)

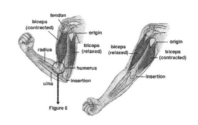

Figure 6

If you know the answer to the original question about one thing a muscle is unable to do, you will automatically know which of the above answers is correct. It may be of little surprise to some readers. Believe it or not, muscles cannot stretch by themselves. They can only contract or shrink. Yes, you can extend or stretch the triceps only when you contract the biceps. What is very important here is that you need to make an effort to relax, which is the key word. By doing this, the triceps will not prevent the smooth bending of the arm. If you fail to relax those particular muscles, bending the arm may be slowed down or even stopped.

I chose the arm as an example above because it is probably the easiest for us to see and feel. Now let me ask you another tricky question. How many muscles do you need to use to stand still like a statue? If you guessed one or two hundred, sorry but you are way off. You may think that because you believe that only the muscles in the legs are needed. OK, what is the answer? Would you believe three hundred? It is true that the body uses three hundred muscles, on average, to balance itself while standing still.

The subject of how we balance and control our posture as we stand is an interesting one. If you are interested in learning more about this subject, there is an in-depth essay entitled "Human Balance and Posture Control during Standing and Walking" by Dr. D.A. Winter (Department of Kinesiology, University of Waterloo, Waterloo, Ontario, Canada), which can be found here: www.cs.cmu.edu/~hgeyer/Teaching/R16-899B/Papers/Winter95Gait&Posture.pdf.

This means that standing still requires nearly half of all the muscles of the body. You may find it difficult to believe or accept this, but have you tried this for ten, or even five, minutes? Think about the special guards at Buckingham Palace or the Martyrs' Shrine in Taiwan. The Queen's Guards have two hours of sentry duty. However, they can march up and down the street after standing still for at least ten to fifteen minutes. The Taiwanese guards have a greater challenge as they must stand and remain still for one full hour. Believe me, this takes more than simple determination. These guards are specially trained for this task.

The reason I chose this second example was to show you the intricacy and complexity of the body management that is required to move or even just keep your balance. Unfortunately, this field is almost totally ignored or unrecognized by many people, including karate practitioners. Training in karate without the proper knowledge of this area tends to result in wasteful, counterproductive, or even harmful movements.

Let's take simple arm movement as an example. If Darwin's theory of evolution is even partially correct, we must have evolved from four-legged mammals. So, imagine that you are a horse or a dog. You use your front legs to reach forward and pull the ground toward you when you walk or run. At the same time, your rear legs are used mainly to push or kick your feet backward to assist with forward motion.

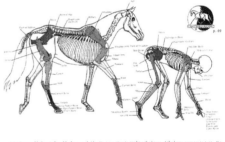

7.2 "Comparable Parts" shared by horse and rider. It's interesting to see how the bones of the horse compare to ours—the exception being that the horse has no collarbones.

We are the only bipedal (two-legged) mammal; thus, we no longer use our arms to walk or run. Since we evolved from four-legged mammal ancestors, such as monkeys or horses, our arms (front legs) have a long but forgotten history of performing a pulling action. This pulling action is how the front legs are used to walk or run. To pull in, you need to use the biceps. Isn't this the unconscious reason many men want to build up and show off their biceps? Therefore, the image of the bent arm with the biceps popping up became a symbol of strength. This is my personal opinion, but I find it very interesting that this phenomenon is quite popular in the Western world.

Pushing the arms forward is not a very difficult movement for humans. On the other hand, walking backward is a difficult task for four-legged mammals. Horses and dogs have to be trained to do this. Walking backward is not as challenging for humans due to the better balance that comes from the mechanics of being bipedal. But, at the same time, we feel that walking backward is not as natural as walking forward. Since we use our arms for more complex tasks than simply walking or running, we can move them forward fairly easily. The action of extending the arm forward is used in pushing and also punching. For this action, you need to use the triceps.

If you had no martial-arts training, the way you would swing your arm to punch someone would most likely be of the roundhouse type. You would swing your fist widely from the outside and try to hit the side of the opponent's head. If you were very observant, you would notice that your fist would end up coming back toward your chest. Try it and you will see how it happens. Interestingly, that is exactly how a cat strikes when it is fighting.

So, what I want to say is that *seiken zuki*, or *choku zuki* (直突き, 'straight punch'), which is commonly used in karate, is an unnatural way of punching. In other words, this kind of punch will not come out naturally. You need training to master this technique. Once you learn it, even *choku zuki* may become natural to you. But, you may remember that your elbow used to stick out during the learning process and that your sensei would point it out and tell you to keep it close to your side. If your elbow deviates from a straight line, this will result in loss of power. In addition, the punch will be more visible to the opponent, which you want to avoid.

Some people do not seem to care about losing power due to misalignment. They tend to rely on their muscles to generate power. Is this wrong? No, it is not completely wrong, but it is not a martial-arts method. In the martial arts, you want the muscles to use the minimum amount of energy to generate the maximum amount of power. You do not want to waste energy. That is the most efficient way to generate power. The martial arts are the most challenging as they are a combination of the most explosive power and the most efficient use of energy. This is like being excellent in both a fifty-meter dash and a marathon at the same time.

If you try to use your muscle power more, you will encounter another potential problem. Trying to create greater muscle power will result in greater tension, which tends to restrict your breathing. In other words, you tend to stop breathing. This will make you tired faster. In the martial arts, you want to keep breathing naturally during a fight. In order to achieve this, you must be in the habit of doing it during your training.

So, you may misunderstand and think I am recommending that you not use your muscles. This is not what I am saying. Of course you need to use your muscles to generate power. What I am saying is that there is a technique that generates great power using a minimal amount of muscle strength. The secret is the title of this chapter. You need to link different parts of the body correctly when you execute a technique. The body parts that need to be linked will differ depending on the technique.

Let's pick an easy example again, a punch. I refer this as being easy not because of the simplicity of the mechanics of the arm or its mobility but rather because of the fact that the movements of the arm are much more visible than those of other parts of the body. Anyway, from *kamae*, you have two choices: *jun zuki* (順突き) with the front arm or *gyaku zuki* with the rear arm. With either option, you still have to move the entire arm straight forward or toward the opponent. During this process, of course, we have to think about the muscles in the arms. As I explained earlier, the triceps must be tense and the biceps must be relaxed. In addition, you are aware that other muscles are involved. For instance, tension of the latissimus dorsi (commonly called the *lat*) at the end of punch is important.

Surprisingly, most people are not aware that many more muscles around the shoulder are involved in this simple arm movement. A couple of the major superficial muscles would be the trapezius and the deltoid. Some of the deeper muscles would be the

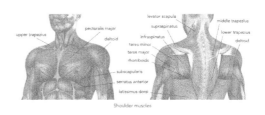

Shoulder muscles

levator scapulae, the rhomboid, the supraspinatus, the subscapularis, the infraspi-
natus, etc. Not only that, there are many muscles around the neck, chest, torso,
and back. I will not name those muscles as you can easily find them, and knowing the names is not that important. What is important is to feel those muscles
and to know which ones need to be tense or relaxed at what moments.

I am sure you have been in a situation where the car in front of you has its
brake lights on continuously. This means the driver is putting his foot on both
the accelerator and the brake at the same time. This comes from either inexperi-
ence or an excessive fear of accidents. You see this in new drivers who have just
passed their driving test or in old drivers who have lost coordination. They are
simply wasting gas and wearing out the brake shoes unnecessarily. It is somewhat
bothersome if such a driver is in front of you, but it is not a crime.

There are many in karate training who are doing just this. They are not relaxing the muscles that are not needed. For instance, many tend to tense the biceps
and even the deltoid and the latissimus dorsi, while the only muscles that need to
be tense (except at the very end) are the triceps.

Even though punching definitely involves the lower half of the body, let's focus on the upper body for now. We will discuss the importance of the lower half
of the body, that is, the stance, later in this chapter. I mentioned the simple motion of the straight punch earlier. Now you are aware that it requires the tensing
and relaxing of large number of muscles. If you tense or relax the wrong muscles
between the hip area and the end of the fist and also have bad timing, you are
either wasting much of your energy or reducing the power of the punch.

In addition to this, the positions of the chin and the head are also important
to the execution of a powerful punch. This requires many muscles around the
neck. More importantly, we must talk about the positioning of the upper body,
including the head. In other words, you can rotate your upper body as you deliver
a punch. This is called *hanmi* (半身, 'half body'). However, you do not want to
overrotate your body. In addition, you want to tilt your upper body toward the
target as you punch in order to put some body weight behind the punch. How-

ever, you do not want to lean in too much and lose your balance. If you lean in too much, the angle of the armpit becomes too wide, and that will result in loss of balance and power.

When you think of your arm, you must pay attention to the shoulder, where two joints, consisting of three major bones, meet. The main joint is a ball-and-socket joint between the shoulder blade (scapula) and the arm bone (humerus). In addition, the collarbone (clavicle) extends across from the sternum to the scapula to form the second joint.

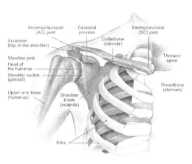

Many readers may believe the humerus is firmly connected to the shoulder blade or the collarbone. Surprisingly, it is not. It is somewhat free and not firmly connected. Due to this loose structure, the shoulder is extremely mobile, which we all know. We can move our arms in many directions and make circular motions. The connection is not as firm as what we find in the hip joint, where the socket is deep (which will be explained in depth later). In fact, the humerus and scapula are connected by seventeen muscles and ligaments. However, the construction allows the arm to hang freely from the shoulder in a sense. This is why we witness many more shoulder injuries than hip injuries.

If you wish to learn more about the structures of the shoulder joint, here is the URL to an article by Oliver Jones: teachmeanatomy.info/upper-limb/joints/shoulder/.

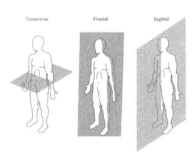

Now, when we think of body mobility, there is a very interesting phrase to consider: *six degrees of freedom* (6DOF). This refers to freedom of movement in a rigid body. According to Techopedia, six degrees of freedom (6DOF) refers to the specific number of axes that a rigid body is able to freely move in three-dimensional space. It defines the number of independent parameters that define the configuration of a mechanical system. Specifically, the body can move in three dimensions, on the X, Y and Z axes, as well as change orientation between those axes through rotation, usually called *pitch*, *yaw* and *roll*. (www.techopedia.com/definition/12702/six-degrees-of-freedom-6dof)

Did you know that those six degrees are required to allow free orientation in space?

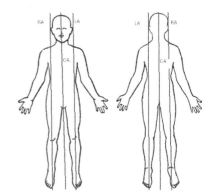

The X, Y, and Z axes are three imaginary lines that dissect the body and create planes of movement (illustration right). The sagittal plane splits the body vertically into the left and right sides. The transverse plane divides the body horizontally into upper and lower sections. The frontal plane runs vertically and divides the body into front and back sides.

In the martial arts, we call these lines *taijiku* (体軸, 'body axes'). The most important body axis is called *seichusen* (正中線, 'center line') or *seichujiku* (正中軸, 'center axis'). In fact, *seichusen* and *seichujiku* are different in the strictest sense of the terms.

Seichusen is the imaginary vertical line that starts from the top of the head and runs through the center of the body, or *seika tanden*, to the *ein* (会陰, 'perineum'). The line does not stop there but extends all the way down to the center point between the ankles. That is the imaginary vertical line that cuts through your body. It is important for keeping your balance when you are standing straight up.

However, you are moving and shifting all the time; thus, you have to think about the *seichujiku*, which is the imaginary line that helps you keep your balance even when you are not standing straight up.

Take a look at the picture of the two dolls on the next page. For your reference, there are two lines. The shorter one designates the *seichusen*, and the longer one designates the *seichujiku*.

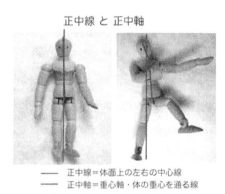

正中線 と 正中軸

——— 正中線＝体面上の左右の中心線
——— 正中軸＝重心軸・体の重心を通る線

The doll on the left shows the position of a human being standing straight up, and you can see how both lines merge in the center of the body. This means the *seichusen* and the *seichujiku* exist at the same location.

Now take a look at the doll on the right. You can see that the figure's left arm and left leg are raised, which means he is off-balance. In order to keep his balance, he has to lean a little to his right—you can see his head tilting to one side. Now the short line and the long line have separated. The short line continues to show the line that divides the body evenly into right and left sides. The long line, however, shows where this figure needs to be in order to keep his balance.

This is why it is critical for all martial artists to be aware of this line, the *seichujiku*. Naturally, you can unconsciously keep your body balanced as you walk, run, sit, etc. However, if you are not only aware of this but also able to manage it, wouldn't you believe that you could manage your body mobility better? I definitely believe so. Superathletes such as Muhammad Ali, Pelé, Maradona, and Michael Jordan displayed superhuman balance and mobility. I am sure they all were able to manage and control the *seichujiku* better than their colleagues and opponents. They might have been prodigies who could control the *seichujiku* unconsciously even if they had never learned the concept. If we martial artists can train while being conscious of this line, I am confident that our performance will improve.

As we discuss this further, we will have to involve this subject. But, for now, let's go back to the punching motion of the arm in relation to the planes of movement in the body. As you can see in the illustration, the arms are located furthest away from the center axis. If we keep the shoulders pointing toward the three- and nine-o'clock positions (no body rotation), we call this *shomen* (正面, 'forward facing'). If we turn or rotate the hips thirty to forty-five degrees, we call this *hanmi* (半身, 'half facing').

Am I the only one who believes that the importance of keeping the body facing forward is overemphasized? I suspect that, at most dojo, you are to assume *hanmi* when you block and *shomen* when you punch. It is OK to teach this to beginners so that they get the basic stances and techniques down. However, once you reach brown belt or above, you must pay more attention to body structure and the connections between the joints in order to produce effective techniques.

If you try to assume *shomen* posture too much, you may pull your punching shoulder back, which is an error that reduces punching power. On the other hand, if you try to extend your arm by turning your hips too much, you may lose your balance, which, of course, reduces the effectiveness of the technique. In both situations, the body structures are off. They are not properly connected. We will investigate further how these connections must be made.

We are still thinking about an effective punch, and we discussed that the arm is connected to the spine via the collarbone and the shoulder blade. Many mistakenly believe that punching power mainly comes from the muscles of the arm and upper body. They also believe power will increase if you rotate your hips, seeing the upper body as one unit. This in and of itself is not a mistake, but such a motion is too visible and is full of wasted energy.

The essence of skillful karate technique is invisibility. In other words, it must produce the maximum amount of power with the minimum amount of body movement. What is important (for the upper body) in the production of power with minimal arm and hip rotation is the role of the spine, or backbone. In addition, the role of the rib cage is also involved. Unfortunately, in karate training, not enough attention is given to either the spine or the rib cage.

When you hear the word *spine*, what image comes to mind? Is it a straight bone or a chain of bones? Most readers probably know that the spine is a structure of small bones. You may even know those small bones are called *vertebrae*.

Then, do you know exactly how many vertebrae make up the spine? Unless you are involved in the medical field or sport science, you most likely do not know or remember the number. Knowing or remembering the exact number itself is not important. However, it is important that instructors know that an average adult has two dozen vertebrae. It is indeed a complex anatomical structure that scaffolds the entire body. It is the main pillar that keeps your body upright.

Even though the details may not be too important for most readers, I want to mention two important facts. One is that the spine is not straight like a stick when you look at it from the side. In fact, you will notice that it has three curves and resembles an S shape (illustration right). These curves help the spine withstand great amounts of stress due to the force of gravity on the body when it adopts an upright posture. The main reason for the S shape is amazing. In fact, the shape functions like a shock absorber. These three sections consist of the cervical vertebrae (seven bones), the thoracic vertebrae (twelve bones) and the lumbar vertebrae (five bones).

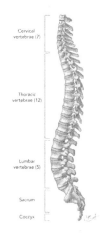

The second important fact about the spine is less well known. Would you believe that the spine has the capacity to move seven different ways? As this is quite important and less recognized among practitioners, I would like to explain it further. Even though your spine is designed to move in seven directions, you must be aware that the degree to which you can actually move in all directions may be limited. This is not a difficult thing to imagine as many of us do experience the challenge of moving our spine in one direction or another. Despite this, I think it is amazing that the human spine has the capacity to do this. OK, here are the seven directions:

1. Flexion (bending forward): This one is very easy to understand.
2. Extension (bending backward): I am sure you understand how this works

and need no explanation.

3/4. Lateral flexion (bending to the right or left): This is side bending. I expect you can imagine this easily and do not need any further explanation.

5/6. Rotation (twisting to the right or left): This ability allows you to rotate the hips when you execute *gyaku zuki*.

7. Axial extension (lengthening): This direction may be the most difficult to imagine. Let me provide some explanation here so that you will have a better idea. When you extend your spine, you are moving through the sagittal plane of movement. Axial extension creates more space between the vertebrae. Sitting up tall from a slouched position is a motion that is considered to be axial extension.

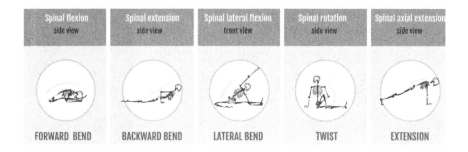

If you are interested and wish to learn more about these seven directions, here is the URL to an article by Ashley Josephine: ashleyjosephine.com/the-7-directions-of-spinal-movement/.

So, when you look at your body structure from the front, you will see that your shoulders are located off-center from the spine, which is the center of the body (illustration right). This results in the swaying of the shoulders as you punch, even if you want to maintain the *shomen* posture throughout the punching process.

Is this a bad thing? The quick answer is yes and no. If you do not know how to connect the sections of the body, as we are discussing here, it is not a good thing as you will lose not only power but also balance. On the other hand, if you are able to execute the technique from the connected position, which I will explain further later on in this chapter, this will provide not only distance but also added power.

If the arms grew out of the area near the spine, we would not need to worry about the possibility of swaying. In fact, I recommend that you bring your fists near the center line (spine) as you execute punches. But, this is another subject, so I will not go further into this. Maybe I will have an opportunity to explain why I recommend this someday in another book.

Oh, I used up a lot of space talking about the spine and failed to touch on the rib cage. Of course, this is not a study of skeletal science, but the body is so amazing, and I feel strongly that we *karateka* should have some basic knowledge of it. Thus, I wish to share some facts about the rib cage for those who are unaware of its unique structure.

Surely, we agree that the rib cage is an important structure as it protects the heart and lungs. The function of most bones, such as those in the arms and legs, is mobility. But, the rib cage has the function of protecting important organs just as the skull protects our brain. However, did you know that, unlike the skull, the rib cage is also mobile? Did you know that it has

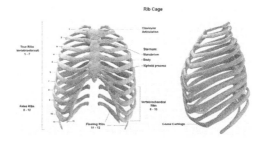

a slight cone shape? Of course you did because it is shaped to store important organs. On the other hand, you may not know that it is flexible, possibly more so than many other sets of bones. Let's find out why and how.

The reason is simple. We need to breathe, and the rib cage must move up and down to allow us to do so. Now we need to see how.

The rib cage consists of long individual bones and joints. In fact, the human rib cage is made up of twelve pairs of rib bones, each pair consisting of a right- and left-side bone, which makes a total of twenty-four bones. These are connected to a single flat bone, the sternum, in the front and to twelve thoracic vertebrae in the back. This construction allows the rib cage to be flexible and movable so that you can breathe better.

One more important and surprising fact is that the maximum rotation angle of the lumbar vertebrae is only five degrees. We know we can turn the hips more when we execute *gyaku zuki*, but this is because the thoracic vertebrae do most of the rotating.

For those who wish to learn more about the rib cage, here is the URL: www. healthline.com/human-body-maps/ribs#1.

Now we are going further with the skeletal structure. The next section may be, I think, the most important part of the body connection. The area I am referring to is the pelvis and the hip joint. In the Japanese martial arts, the pelvis area, or *seika tanden*, is widely considered to be the most important area to train and develop. Of course, the *seika tanden* is not a bone or a muscle. I will not go deeply into a definition or explanation of the *seika tanden* here. Instead, I need to emphasize that it is not a coincidence that the *seika tanden* happens to be in the area of the pelvis.

PELVIS

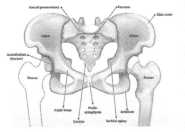

Let's look at some facts about this basin-shaped bone structure, the pelvis (illustration left). Firstly, it is located at the base of the spine. Secondly, it forms the sockets of the hip joints, which will be discussed further a little later. Though the pelvis looks like one unit, it is, in fact, made up of three parts: the hip bones, the sacrum, and the coccyx. Then, the hip bones are made up of three bones. I will list them here, though remembering these names is not important for most of us. They are the ilium, the ischium, and the pubis. I wanted to cover this much just to show that this section is not simple but rather very complex.

What are the functions of the pelvis? We know that it contains the intestines, the bladder, and the internal sex organs. We also know that it connects the trunk and the legs. More important to our conversation, the pelvis supports and balances the trunk. Now, this is a very important fact, and I will need to come back

to this after all of the connections have been explained. The pelvis forms the sockets of the hip joints
in order to connect the trunk and the legs. As you can
see in the illustration to the right, each socket is deep,
unlike the one for the shoulder, and the ball of the
femur (thigh bone) fits in securely. This construction
is natural and necessary as you depend on your two

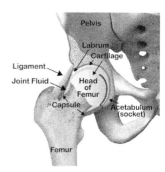

legs not only to stand but to walk, run, etc. If your leg were to slip from your hip
often, you would have a serious handicap in your daily activities. The hip is the
second-largest weight-bearing joint next to the knee. This is why many senior
citizens and some *karateka* experience hip-joint problems.

The natural advantage of the hip joint is its stability. This is not only because
of its deep socket but also because of the many ligaments and muscles that connect the ball of the femur securely to the socket. This is the reason you feel that
the kick is very securely locked in when you execute *yoko geri kekomi* (横蹴り
蹴込み). Even though the hip joint is very dynamic and designed to mobilize
the lower extremity, there is a limitation to its mobility. It is not as mobile as the
shoulder joint. After practicing *yoko geri kekomi* and *yoko geri keage* (横蹴り
蹴上げ) for many years, many senior *karateka* experience hip-joint problems.
Some, sadly, have to have their hip joints replaced. Many older people (non-
karateka) in their seventies and eighties also experience hip-joint problems. This
comes from wearing out the joint through many years of walking and other leg
activities.

Let's take a look at the five directions of the
hip joint (illustration right).

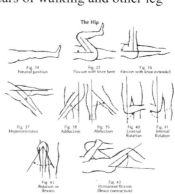

1. Flexion (raising the leg forward 110
    to 130 degrees): The range of flexion
    increases as you relax the hamstring
    muscles.

2. Extension (bringing the leg backward 30 degrees): This motion is limited compared to flexion.

3. Abduction (moving the leg laterally inside and outside 20 to 30 degrees): This motion is used to execute *yoko geri*.

4. Lateral, or external, rotation (moving the knee and foot outwardly 45 degrees)

5. Medial, or internal, rotation (moving the knee and foot inwardly 40 degrees)

As you can see, the hip joint is less mobile than the shoulder joint as the former has only five directions, while the latter enjoys seven. Another fact that stands out is that the degree of mobility of abduction is the least among the five directions. While flexion can go as high as 130 degrees, abduction is only 30 degrees. This is why it is easier to execute *jodan mae geri* than *jodan yoko geri*. Practicing many *mae geri* will not cause hip-joint problems as often as practicing *yoko geri* in large numbers.

Now let us go down to the legs. As you know, we need our legs to stand up and to move around. In general, we can consider the lower extremities to consist of five parts: foot, ankle, lower leg, knee, and thigh. Out of these five parts, the

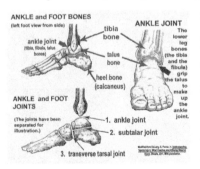

ankle and the knee are joints. The most complex structure is the foot, which has twenty-six bones. The skeletal structure of the foot is similar to that of the hand, but it is built stronger due to the body weight it must bear. At the same time, though it can make some complex moves, the foot is less mobile and less

maneuverable than the hand, which is easy to guess. The function of the foot is very interesting and important to our mobility, but I will not go into the details of the foot in this chapter. I wrote about this in Chapter 13: "The Mystery of the Arch" of my book *Karatedo Paradigm Shift*.

The foot is connected to the lower part of the leg via the ankle. I will not go too deeply into the functions of the ankle, but it consists of two parts: the upper ankle and the lower ankle. The upper ankle allows the foot to move upward, downward, and a little to the side. Though it does not move as much as the upper ankle, it still has an important function. The lower ankle allows the foot to tilt to the side as well as to turn inward and outward. This function is necessary for us to take a normal step forward and backward.

Now we need to take a look at the second joint, the knee, which is also a very important mechanism. You may be aware that it is a hinge joint, which means it bends back and forth on a single plane. Thus, the main function of the knee is to act as a hinge for the lower

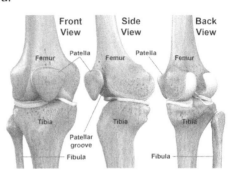

extremity. Interestingly, the knee does not only bend back and forth. There are also rotational movements at the knee joint.

An article by Jonathan Cluett, MD, entitled "Anatomy of the Knee" lists the following important functions of the knee:

- Lower extremity support when standing
- Strength and power with movements such as standing up, squatting, or climbing
- Efficient movement when walking or running
- Power to propel your body more when you move
- Shock absorption when walking or landing from a jumping position

These are only the main functions that the knee joint performs. If you wish to enable any of these functions to operate normally, certainly, all of the complex structures, including but not limited to the bones, ligaments, cartilage, and muscles, need to be working harmoniously as a team.

If you wish to read and learn more about the anatomy of knee, here is the URL: www.verywellhealth.com/knee-anatomy-2549239.

Now that we have touched on almost all of the muscles, bones, and joints that are necessary to stand, move, and throw a punch, let's return to the main subject of connecting our body. We agree that all of these bones and joints are loosely connected with muscles and ligaments. If they were more tightly connected like a machine, you would move like a robot. Thanks to the numerous joints and muscles, you can move very fluidly.

When you walk, or even run, you are not aware and do not think that you are coordinating and balancing all of these joints and muscles to produce such motions. When you run fast, you may consciously try to bring your knees up higher as this will increase your speed. You may even try to swing your arms faster and in bigger circles. However, that is about all you will think about your body elements.

On the other hand, if you were an Olympic runner, you would look at your body differently. You would pay much more attention to how you used your feet and legs. The position of your upper body would become critical to you. You would strengthen the necessary muscles. You might ask the coach to monitor your running posture, check your blood pressure, etc.

You may say, "OK, I understand that an Olympic athlete would pay much more attention to his body. But, what has that got to do with me, an average karate practitioner?" To this question, I must emphatically claim that mastering karate is as challenging as becoming an Olympic athlete, if not more so. You may not easily agree with this statement. However, ask yourself how many true karate masters you have seen. I am not talking about tournament champions or someone who breaks many boards with a single punch. I am talking about experts, possibly in their seventies or eighties, who can deliver a one- or zero-inch punch, move ever so fluidly and beautifully, and use their arms like a whip, etc. You are lucky if you have met one such person in your karate journey. Just like an Olympic athlete, it takes many years of hard training (not only physical but also mental and spiritual) to achieve this level of true expertise.

Such expertise can be achieved only when you learn and master the perfect

connection of your body parts. I am aware it is difficult to imagine such a connection if you have not thought about it and tried it yourself. Let me give you one
example that could sort of give you the feeling of the connection. Imagine that

you are standing and you wish to jump
very high. Can you jump if you only
swing your arms upward? Of course
not. You need to bend your knees and
use your legs to jump. We all know
this. Then, how about if you jump

while keeping your upper body upright? I am sure you would bend your upper
body forward and then swing it upward with your arms. You would also add your
back and arm muscles to jump higher.

You also know that there is a specific sequence of motions to the body parts.
You do not move them all at one time. First, you bend your knees. Simultaneously, you bend your upper body by forty-five or closer to ninety degrees with
your arms poised down and a little toward the back. Though the jump may look
like a single body motion, the power starts from your feet. Just stand and position yourself as if ready to jump. You will feel the tight connection of your feet
to the floor, and you may feel the tightening of your toes followed by that of the
knees and the leg muscles. Almost simultaneously, you push your hips forward
and tense the back muscles to lift your upper body. At the same time, you use the
upswing of your arms to aid the upward lift. In addition, you may learn to relax
your upper body before the jump, and you may incorporate the explosive exhalation of your breath. All of the parts—feet, knees, legs, hips, back, arms, and many
other muscles—must work together in a specific sequence. If any part of the
sequence is off or out of sync, your jump will not be as high as it can be.

This is exactly the same when you execute a karate technique. As an easy
example, let's take a punch, say *gyaku zuki*. So, let us imagine that you are standing in front of a *makiwara*, and you are going to punch it with *gyaku zuki*. Now,
if you stand in *heiko dachi* (平行, 'parallel stance') and only move your arms to

punch the target, this will be very similar to your effort to jump using only the arm swing. A large hip rotation is encouraged when executing *gyaku zuki*. Yes, it will help. However, you will be surprised to find how little the hip joints can turn. Without the cooperation of the legs, they can turn only ten to fifteen degrees. I am sure you will claim that you can rotate your hips much more. What you are saying is true, but you are increasing the range of motion by using knee and ankle rotations. So, you must use everything in your legs just to rotate your hips.

As you get yourself ready to execute *gyaku zuki*, you get into *zenkutsu dachi*. You bring your punching fist to your hip and extend the other arm forward. Are your arms tense? If you are a senior practitioner, you will most likely say no. Yes, just like when you want to jump, it is better to keep the upper body relaxed when you are preparing for action. Then, you turn your hips and bring the punching side back. At this point, what part of the body are you paying the most attention to? Of course you are gazing at the *makiwara* as that is your target. At the same time, the body part you want to pay the most attention to is your legs, particularly your feet at first. If you are an experienced practitioner, you may even feel the particular parts of your feet. Then, you check the position of your knees as you know that an incorrect position could result in a poor punch. You make sure you have a correct *zenkutsu dachi*. To do this, you have to check the position and the form of your legs and joints, mainly your knees and hips.

So, how many main parts are there between your feet and your punching fist? In a strict sense, we cannot consider the foot to be one piece as it consists of many joints at the toes, ligaments, and muscles; however, we will do so in this example just to make it simple. By the way, I find our feet to be an incredible masterwork. OK, let's get back to what we were discussing.

So, to look at the body connection, we must start from the bottom of the body, the feet. The connected parts that follow are the ankle, shin, knee, thigh, pelvis/hips (including the joints), lower torso, and upper torso (including the entire back and the shoulders). From the shoulder joint, we move to the upper arm, elbow, forearm, wrist, and, finally, the punching fist. Here again, a fist consists of five fingers and many joints, ligaments, muscles, etc. So, it is hardly one part, but we will consider it as such for the purposes of this discussion.

OK, I count fourteen major parts. As I mentioned earlier, some of the parts, such as the feet and the joints, consist of many subparts, so there are many more than a mere fourteen. Despite this, I think it is still a complex mechanism even if the number of parts is fourteen. You are incredible as you learn how to coordinate these various parts and move either in unison or in sequence to produce the kind of result you wish. It must work like falling dominoes. Imagine that one

domino fails to fall. It will stop the entire cascading motion in the middle. It is visible, so you can easily see it.

I must caution you here not to think that your body works exactly like falling dominoes. In other words, it is not a systematic sequence of movements. Your body is a million times more complex than a domino system. I brought this simple example up so that you could visualize how all of the parts must work and how there would be a problem if even one single piece did not work properly or were out of sync. Unfortunately, it is not so easy to see how your body parts work. This is exactly why it is so difficult not only to understand this mechanism but also to learn how to do it correctly.

The power starts from the feet, and we describe it as receiving energy from the ground. Then, it rises up to your leg, initially your lower leg, which is the shin part. It is enhanced a little by your ankle and knee joints. Believe it or not, a tiny vibration is produced in your legs as the energy travels through them. Then, as it passes through the largest joint, which is your hip joint, it gets magnified more and is aided by a slight hip rotation. Finally, the major power enhancement occurs with the undulation of your torso, powered by your back and belly muscles.

What happens next is a release of the power. Your arm must be totally relaxed and must travel smoothly forward, transcending the power generated toward the target. What happens if you squeeze a bottle of ketchup very quickly and strongly? You know that the contents, the ketchup, will shoot out if you do this. Well, the power of your punch should be like this at the end. All of the energy generated by your lower, central, and upper torso must be shot out successfully. During this process, the muscles in your arm and shoulder must not hinder the transfer of energy. This is why your arm must be totally relaxed.

 Think of your body as a large orchestra with hundreds of different instruments. In order to play beautiful music, every instrument must be in tune. Not only that, every musician must do his part correctly. If a drum makes a loud sound at the wrong time, it will ruin the whole piece. An excellent conductor can detect when any musician is behind or off. The musicians must play according to the correct speed, sequence, timing, etc. Here again, this is only a simple analogy to help you visualize the importance of teamwork and timing.

This is what you must do within your body. A clock can do this as it is a machine. But, this is extremely difficult for your body. We want to believe we can manage our body parts precisely, but that is not the case for most of us. It takes a lot of training to achieve this. But, first of all, you must know how to do it. Even if you have an excellent instructor who knows how to do it, he will have a difficult time showing you or making it possible for you to copy it.

I feel that I need to write more to explain what you need to do to connect your body parts. On the other hand, I feel that the more I explain, the further I get from a complete understanding. I must apologize as this may be due to my poor ability to explain.

I encounter this often when I want to explain a karate technique. Some

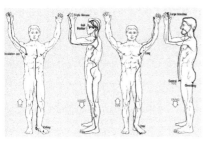

techniques and concepts are fairly easy to explain and can be understood. Then, there are others that are extremely difficult, such as ki and the one-inch punch. I am afraid the concept of connecting the body or body parts is one of these. Just like ki, proper connection of the body can be understood only when you can demonstrate it with your own body. It may sound like a cop-out, but, sadly, this is true. However, I do not wish to just leave you in the dark. Let me give you a few more hints about what you can try during your training in order to achieve the proper connection.

First of all, you must keep your body, particularly your upper body, including your torso and your arms, very relaxed. In Shotokan, the concept of *kime* (極め), or total body tension, is so valued and so often practiced that it results in excessive tension throughout all the techniques of *kata* and *kumite*. Remember that a whip is very flexible and loose before you swing it and strike with it.

Another example may be an old toy I used to have when I was a child. It is a bamboo snake (photo right). Multiple parts of it are connected and painted green, usually to make it look like a snake. You hold the tail part and shake or swing it, mainly

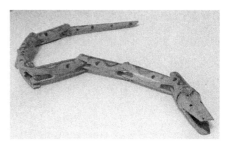

sideways. Then, it moves in a way that is similar to the way a real snake would slither. The parts are connected, but only loosely so that they can move easily. It requires a smooth twisting motion of your hand, wrist, and arm to make the loosely connected parts move in a certain way so that it looks like the motion of a snake.

Secondly, try to point your rear knee downward and not too far to the outside when you punch. When you are getting ready to punch, of course, you need to relax your rear leg. At that moment, your knee may point somewhat outward. When you punch, you squeeze the inner muscles of both thighs. This brings your rear knee down. The front knee must be pointed toward the target. As you rotate your hip, your knee and your entire upper body will move slightly forward.

Thirdly, do not depend on hip rotation. Yes, this may be another concept that goes against what you have learned before. Surprisingly, hip rotation is not what generates the power of the punch. It is, more or less, only the initial power, the power that connects the ground energy (your feet and legs) to your upper body. What you need to do is prevent major hip rotation. Rotate only within the natural hip movement, maybe ten or fifteen degrees, and no more. In fact, if you rotate too much, it will reduce the energy that is being transferred from your lower body.

The energy that has been transferred from your foot, leg, and hip parts is magnified mostly when it travels through your upper body. The punch should not depend on the muscles of your arm, or even those of the shoulder region. All of your back muscles, with the help of your frontal muscles, are what power the punch just like the thong part of a whip. In this whip analogy, your feet and legs are the handle, your hips are the transition knot, your punching arm is the fall, and, finally, your fist is the popper.

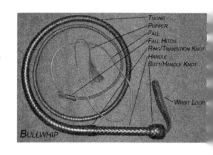

One thing you must remember is that the transition is from the foot area; however, it is so fast that you may not feel the transition to the fist, initially. Those parts are made up of hundreds of muscles, as well as many bones and ligaments. Each one of these must ignite independently or in unison with other parts. This is something you must feel and cannot be taught. The hint is that it is a very tiny vibration of the muscles, like the vibration of a team of violins in an orchestra. The mysterious but challenging part of this technique is that the vibration does not move in just one direction. There are some up-and-down and forward-and-backward motions. In other words, a fine tuning of tension and relaxation must happen within your body.

My final suggestion for those readers who are seriously interested in this concept and technique is to study physiology and kinesiology. You must learn the details and construction of your body parts and understand how they work. I think this will help you appreciate this concept and, hopefully, achieve this technique.

All of us have such a wonderful and sophisticated tool that we call *our body*. At the same time, we take it for granted and do not know too much about it. Unfortunately, only a few can tune it perfectly and realize its excellent potential. I strongly believe that, by training in karate correctly, you can achieve this miracle. Would you not like to be one of the few?

CHAPTER SIXTEEN
第十六章

THE PARADOXES OF BUJUTSU
武術のパラドックスとは？

You might be perplexed when you see the title of this chapter. I am happy if it made you curious. In fact, I believe there are two big paradoxes in Japanese *bujutsu* (武術, 'martial arts'), including kenjutsu and kyudo. Interestingly, the paradoxes I present here also apply to karate, a martial art without weapons. Let's walk through this interesting and often ignored subject.

What is interesting is that the facts presented here are well known, yet many people typically do not consider them to be paradoxical or unnatural. I hope my opening made you very curious to find out what these facts are. Let me present my case and ask the reader to judge if it makes any sense.

Paradox One

The use of the term *martial art* means that we teach and practice techniques to maim, and even kill, our opponents.

Is maiming or killing a person a good thing? I am sure you will strongly deny this. Then, are we teaching the students at our dojo how to be criminals? Of course we are not. It is illegal to take action without a cause. On the other hand, we are allowed to use necessary force when we must defend ourselves.

I find it interesting that, despite the fact that beating up or cutting a person who is just passing by on the street is a criminal act, we are allowed to teach such a skill and a martial-arts sensei is well respected for doing so. We think nothing of the fact that we are teaching and learning killing techniques because we know that we are doing it for self-defense purposes.

I am sure you agree that the main purpose of learning and practicing armed *bujutsu*, such as kenjutsu, iaido, and kyudo, nowadays is not usually self-defense. We are not allowed, in many countries, to carry a real sword as we step outside our house to go to work or go shopping. The practitioners of those arts train for other purposes, such as discipline and mental training. Learning how to shoot a

pistol may be quite different as this is mainly learned for self-defense purposes. However, pistol shooting is not Japanese *budo*, so I will not include it in this discussion.

The legality is the same when it comes to learning or teaching how to cut a person with a sword. However, there is a big difference between karate and kenjutsu or iaido. This can become a sticky situation for karate practitioners. In kenjutsu, of course, you must use a tool or a weapon (a sword) to harm another person. In karate, on the other hand, you do not need any tool because your body is a weapon. If a karate practitioner has to defend himself using his karate skill and knocks his opponent out, he needs to worry about being sued due to the fact that he knew karate and might have retaliated too excessively.

In fact, one karate weapon, the nunchaku (ヌンチャク), is even illegal to purchase or own in a couple of U.S. states and some Western countries. As you know, most nunchaku are only a pair of wooden

or plastic sticks. There are nunchaku made from steel and other metals, but they are not popular as they are much heavier (except for the light aluminum ones that are used for demonstration purposes). It is very strange and unfair that not only carrying a pair of wooden sticks but also purchasing them is illegal. On the other hand, it is quite legal to purchase and carry a pistol or high-powered gun in most states in the USA. This is an interesting subject, which we will touch on in the second paradox.

Paradox Two

We all know that we are living in a world of high-tech weapons, including missiles, rockets, and nuclear bombs. On the other hand, *bujutsu* is a practice that utilizes ancient weapons, such as swords and spears. Karate is even less advanced as it consists of hand-to-hand combat. According to *Merriam-Webster's Collegiate Dictionary, Eleventh Edition, karate* is defined as follows: "a Japanese art of self-defense employing hand strikes and kicks to disable or subdue an opponent."

Isn't it amazing that some *bujutsu*, such as judo and karate, are becoming popular in a world of nuclear bombs? Judo was accepted into the Olympic Games

in 1964. Karate, too, debuted in the 2021 Tokyo Olympics. The popularity of karate in particular is at an all-time high. According to one study, the worldwide population of karate, believe it or not, has now surpassed one hundred million. This figure is almost unbelievable.

Comparing the use of a nuclear weapon to karate may be too extreme. It is a fact, however, that we live in a world where, at least in most countries, guns are very popular and common. Here are some statistics to show the pervasiveness of firearms in the USA. According to an article in *The Guardian*, U.S. citizens

own at least 265 million firearms. This means there is about one gun for every American citizen, including babies. The U.S. is by far the number-one country when it comes to owning guns. A distant second is Yemen, with about fifty-five guns for every one hundred people.

Here is the full article on the gun numbers for those who are interested in knowing the details: www.theguardian.com/us-news/2017/nov/15/the-gun-numbers-just-3-of-american-adults-own-a-collective-133m-firearms.

In the country where karate originated, Japan, there is also gun violence each year, though far less than in most Western countries. According to Nippon.com, the National Police Agency announced that there were only twenty-two shooting crimes in 2017. Members of organized crime syndicates, or yakuza, were the perpetrators of thirteen of those crimes. Amazingly, only three people were killed, and five were injured.

Here is the full article on gun crimes in Japan: www.nippon.com/en/features/h00178/.

Even if you are an expert in karate, your chances of survival in a fight against an opponent with a gun, or even a knife, are much lower than when you have a gun in your hand. Some karate and martial-arts instructors teach their students how to defend themselves in a fight against an opponent who is armed with a knife or a gun. It is my personal opinion that what they are doing is quite ir-

responsible if they believe an amateur will be able to execute those techniques in a real street fight or holdup situation. Even if you have trained in those techniques for several years, I do not think it is a wise idea to risk your life fighting against an armed assailant.

Against an opponent with a knife or a gun, I recommend that my students not fight back but rather give up their wallet and other valuables in order to save their lives. Such an act is not cowardice but rather a wise choice and an excellent self-defense tactic. The stupidest thing is to become a dead "hero" when the assailant is demanding only material things.

Of course, it is a totally different story if the opponent is threatening your life or the life of your loved ones. You have to fight to protect your life and that of your loved ones. But, how many times do you think you will be in that situation in your life? Typically, a robber or a gang member would not risk his life to assault you. If you show that you are willing to fight to the death, you will be able to intimidate him and get him to back down. To do this, judo or karate skill is not required. What is required is your attitude and posture.

Then, why is the popularity of karate and judo increasing around the world, including in Japan? As I mentioned earlier, I do not think judo or karate techniques can be a sufficient weapon of self-defense against an opponent with a gun. Is the popularity increasing because the average citizen believes otherwise? I do not think so. I believe people are looking at *bujutsu*, and at karate particularly, for different reasons.

For children, I hear two major reasons. One is that the parents want their children to learn karate so that they will not be easily bullied. The other is that the parents want the kids to learn discipline and etiquette.

When you ask adult practitioners why they started to practice karate, you will find something very interesting. Other than those whose parents forced them to take karate, the most frequent reason is that they wanted to look like Bruce Lee or Jackie Chan. The kung fu movies from the seventies and eighties had a great impact on the youth of that time. Mainly, young boys wanted to be a kung fu master just as much as they dreamt of becoming Superman. While Superman is totally fictitious, a kung fu master seems realistic.

Of course, after training in karate, most of us realized that the superhuman kung fu or karate master is also fictitious. However, this did not stop us from

training as we discovered other values, such as respect, perseverance, courage, honor, etc. I am sure I do not need to elaborate as many readers have experienced what I have described above.

I want to conclude this short chapter with the final paradox of karate. *Te*, the old name for karate used on Okinawa, originated hundreds of years ago. During the time of the samurai, the Okinawans had to develop hand-to-hand combat techniques. At that time, they were literally fighting for their lives. Now, in the twenty-first century, while we are enjoying a more peaceful life, karate is

becoming more and more popular. It is not because karate can be used in a street fight but mainly because it is a fun sport. Karate matches these days are totally safe and have all kinds of protectors. Competitors are allowed to use only safe techniques. Dangerous techniques, such as poking the eyes or kicking the groin, are prohibited, and competitors can lose a match for using such techniques.

Karate originated from bare-handed killing techniques and was practiced only by a select few samurai and palace guards. Karate in the twenty-first century has become a very safe and fun activity enjoyed by millions of people. If the ancient karate masters who created *te* with their sweat and blood could see this unbelievable popularity, I am not sure if they would be happy or bless this "development."

What do you think? No matter what your answer may be, I consider this gap to be the biggest paradox of karate.

CHAPTER SEVENTEEN
第十七章

THE SECRET OF BREATHING METHODS
呼吸法の秘密

We all know breathing is important. It is probably the most important thing for our survival. Water and food are also important, but we can survive for a week without food and maybe one or two days without water. On the other hand, most of us would not survive if there were no air for us to breath for more than two minutes. Many of us cannot hold our breath or stay underwater for even one minute.

I suspect the reader will agree that breathing is considered to be extremely important in martial-arts training, which, of course, includes karate. We all know that proper breathing is necessary for proper *kime*. Not being able to maintain good breathing causes you to get tired very quickly in your training. Senior practitioners also know that it is important to hide their breathing from their opponents. By doing this, they can keep their intentions and techniques undetected.

Benefits of Breath Training

But, do you know the full extent of the benefits of breathing exercises? There is a good article that you should read on this topic. It's entitled "9 Benefits of Breath Training" and is written by Chad Schwab of South Africa, who is a serious athlete specializing in surfing and boxing. Here is the URL if

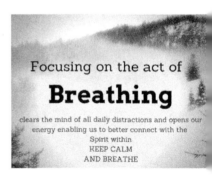

you're interested: www.tickettoridegroup.com/blog/9-benefits-breath-training/.

Here are the nine benefits listed by Schwab in his article:

1. Have the lung capacity of a whale
2. Increase your cardio strength
3. Perform better, recover faster
4. The mental game

5. Decrease stress
6. Increase your anaerobic threshold
7. Handle higher levels of carbon dioxide
8. Increase oxygen in the body
9. Increase your immune system

Now that you have seen these benefits, I bet you are wondering how you can use breathing exercises more seriously in order to experience them in your own karate training and in your daily life.

In fact, there are many different ways of breathing. They teach this in yoga, tai chi, and Zen meditation. On the other hand, sadly, I have not seen much teaching on this important subject in the karate dojo I have visited so far. Despite the importance of this subject, only a few sensei seem to know how to teach it. Apparently, their teachers did not teach them how to train, exercise, or control their breathing. It is a shame, so I wish to contribute my knowledge and, hopefully, shed some light on this seemingly ignored or forgotten subject.

Hi no Kokyu

As I mentioned earlier, there are many different ways to breathe and many different exercise methods. Basically, you control your breathing by four different actions. Most readers know about inhalation and exhalation. However, few are aware of the importance of holding their breath as part of a breathing exercise. There are two holding actions. One is holding after inhalation, and the other is holding after exhalation.

Of course, there are several breathing meth-

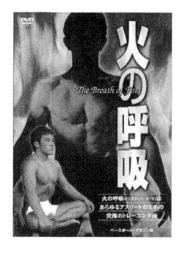

ods that do not involve holding your breath. These methods can be achieved by increasing or decreasing the length of time used for inhalation and exhalation. One of these methods is *hi no kokyu* (火の呼吸, 'fire breathing'), which is found in yoga and Shugendo (修験道).

According to Encyclopedia.com, Shugendo is explained as follows:

> Shugendō is a syncretistic Japanese Buddhist tradition of mountain ascetic practices that incorporates elements from shamanism, indigenous Japanese folk beliefs concerning mountains and spirits of the dead, and Daoist magic. The word *Shugendō* literally translates as 'the way of cultivating supernatural power'. Its practitioners are known as *yamabushi* (those who "lie down" in the mountains) or *shugenja* (ascetics, or "those who cultivate power"). Although their role has evolved and changed over the years, these figures were expected to accumulate religious power by undergoing severe ascetic practices in the mountains, such as fasting, meditating, reciting spells or Buddhist texts, sitting under waterfalls, gathering firewood, abstaining from water, hanging over cliffs to "weigh" one's sins, retiring in solitary confinement to caves, and performing rituals such as fire ceremonies. *Shugenja* then drew on this power to provide services, such as guiding pilgrims, performing religious rites, and demonstrating superhuman feats like walking on fire, as well as divination, exorcism, and prayers.

If you are interested in the history and the full explanation, here is the URL

to the encyclopedia: www.encyclopedia.com/religion/encyclopedias-almanacs-transcripts-and-maps/shugendo.

Hi no kokyu became famous, at least in Japan, when Rickson Gracie (1958–), the well-known champion of Brazilian Jujutsu (photo right), revealed more than ten years ago that this rapid breathing method was part of his training menu. Here is a short video of his yoga training, which includes this breathing exercise: www.youtube.com/

watch?v=CB_KRHXU1BA.

However, we will not go into *hi no kokyu* or any other sophisticated breathing method here. Here I wish to share one very simple exercise method that anyone can do to improve his breathing. You will find out how by reading this chapter, but you need to train almost daily for many months, just as you do with karate training. I cannot overemphasize that it will require consistent (almost daily) training to acquire this new breathing technique.

Even if you do not or cannot continue for many months, I am pretty confident that there are many useful hints in this chapter that will improve your breathing method.

Nose Breathing

Let me give you a few improvement ideas that you can acquire right away. One is to inhale (almost always) through your nose during your breath training. Of course, you want to do this in your daily life, as well. Breathing through your mouth is highly discouraged mainly due to health reasons. You want to limit breathing through your mouth if your nose is congested or during strenuous training.

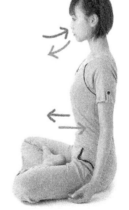

According to information found on the Optimal Breathing website (founded by Michael Grant White, a California state certified nutrition consultant and North Carolina licensed massage and bodywork therapist), nose breathing does the following:

- Helps fight infections
- Ensures better blood flow and lung volumes
- Helps to maintaining body temperature
- Helps in better brain functions

- Helps during your workouts

On the other hand, mouth breathing does the following:

- Gives deadly bacteria free entry through your mouth
- Weakens your lungs, heart, etc.
- Extends an open invitation to snoring or sleep apnea
- Causes constriction of blood vessels
- Restricts your enjoyment of smelling
- Can affect your appearance

You can read the entire explanation of these symptoms and benefits at the following URL: https://optimalbreathing.com/pages/nose-breathing.

Breath Holding

Earlier in this chapter, I pointed out that there are four functions, or stages, of breathing. We are very aware of inhalation and exhalation. What we tend to forget or ignore are the two types of breath holding. Incredibly, the holding actions are as important as the other two.

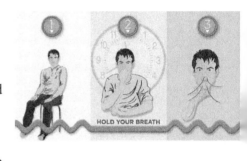

Some may ask which holding action is the more important of the two. That is a fair question, but it depends on what you are trying to achieve. I will not go into

the details in this chapter, but I can say that both are almost equally important.

There is an interesting article by Stig Severinsen (photo left) entitled "Develop Mental Power with Breath Holding." Severinsen is the founder of Breatheology and holds not only an MS in biology but also a PhD in medicine and is also a four-time free-diving world champion and a Guinness World Record holder. He is also the author of *Breatheology: The Art of Conscious Breathing* (Idelson Gnocchi Publishers, Ltd., 2010). Severinsen's article can be found at www.breatheology.com/mental-powers-breath-holding/.

In his article, Severinsen claims that holding your breath provides the following:

- More energy
- Calmness
- Resilience to stress
- Mental stability
- Greater focus on priorities and goals
- Closer connection to the body
- More attention to the moment

He also makes the claim that, in the long run,

meditation and breath holds seem to develop your nervous system and brain. Scientific studies have revealed that people who practice meditation and/or freediving show marked changes in their brain and nervous system. One area in the nervous system that undergoes changes lies in the brain stem and is connected to the vagus nerve. This is part of the calming parasympathetic pathway which counteracts stress.

Long Breathing

Now you have learned some basic ideas about breathing, and I believe we can jump into the breathing method. But, before that, do you know how many times you breathe per minute? This is your respiratory rate, and it is such a simple thing to figure out.

Thus, it seems all of us should know. However, as far as I know, not too many people bother to measure this or test their breathing cycles. If you do not know the exact data on your breathing, please take a few minutes and find out, on average, how many breathing cycles you go through per minute.

According to the Cleveland Clinic, an adult breathes an average of twelve to twenty times per minute. If you are an athlete or a karate black belt, your numbers are probably lower than that. By doing breath training, you train to have fewer breathing cycles per minute, which means you breathe longer in the process. Quick, short breaths are not a sign of good health. I am sure you have seen sick and obese people exhibiting that type of breathing. Zen meditation uses slow breathing, which is for the improvement of both mental and physical health. If you have been in a Zen meditation or yoga class, I am sure you learned how to take slower, longer breaths. Here you do not need to do the meditation. You can sit casually either in a chair or on the floor.

The Cleveland Clinic has a very interesting article entitled "Vital Signs," which includes a section on respiratory rate. I will share the URL here: my.clevelandclinic.org/health/articles/10881-vital-signs.

Breath-Training Steps

Here are the simple steps I suggest to improve or extend your breathing:

Step 1

Check your breathing cycles to see how many times you normally breathe per minute. If you are breathing two times or fewer per minute, you can jump to Step 5. However, most readers will find that they

THE SKILL of BREATHING
5 Breathing Techniques
to Improve Health

breathe ten times or more per minute. You want to reduce this number, but you must do it gradually.

Step 2

What you need to do is cut your breathing cycle down to eight times per minute (unless you are already at that level). Eight cycles per minute means you take seven to eight seconds per breathing cycle. To make it easier to calculate, let's take eight seconds for one cycle. What you need to do is allocate the same time for inhalation and exhalation. In other words, you need to inhale for four seconds and exhale for four seconds, as well. This should not be too difficult to do. At this level, you do not need to introduce a breath-holding period.

What is difficult is making this cycle permanent. Unless you train your breathing habits regularly and teach your body the proper breathing time, the cycle will shorten, and you will return to breathing faster. This is why it is a good idea to combine the breathing exercise with meditation. Though it is optional, closing your eyes and trying to think less allows you to focus on your breathing much more easily. I suggest you do this every day

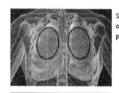

Shallow breathing only fills the top part of the lungs.

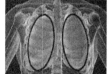

Deep breathing fills the lungs fully!

More air = more oxygen = improved health and energy.

for one month if possible. This is like karate training, so the minimum frequency for your breathing exercises should be no lower than three to four times per week. If you do not have much free time during the day, you can do this while you are in bed, either right before you go to sleep or right after you wake up.

Step 3

If you become comfortable with eight times per minute, extend your breathing and try four times per minute. In this case, you will use about fifteen seconds for one breathing cycle, in which you will spend the same amount of time for inhalation and exhalation, but you may also want to introduce a breath-holding period. The desired amount of time for each section of the breathing cycle (inhalation, exhalation, and holding) is five seconds. Initially, however, you may find it difficult to hold your breath that long. In that case, you can reduce the amount of holding time, say, down to three seconds. The time for inhalation and exhalation will, of course, then be extended to six seconds each to keep the total cycle time at fifteen seconds. When you become comfortable doing this breathing at those intervals for one hour or longer, then you can increase the holding time to five seconds or even longer.

Just as you did in Step 2, you need to train your breathing habits as often as possible for at least one month or until you feel comfortable doing the breathing cycle as described above. Of course, if reducing it to four times per minute is too challenging, you can reduce it to six times instead. This is much more gradual and will be easier to adopt. However, the time required to reach the ultimate goal will be pushed further out, and you will need more patience and a greater degree of commitment as you will have to take more steps.

Step 4

If you are successful at four times per minute, you are ready to reduce it to three times per minute. Though cutting down from four to three might seem easy, you will find that the degree of difficulty increases exponentially.

At three cycles per minute, you will complete one cycle every twenty seconds. You can divide the three functions equally into approximately seven seconds each.

There are three different ways of breathing. The first one is the pattern of exhalation, inhalation, and holding. The second is that of inhalation, exhalation, and holding. These two seem to be similar, and you may not see the difference. However, if you try them, you will find that the second method is harder than the first one. In other words, it is much easier to hold your breath after you fill your lungs with the air. The other way requires you to hold the breath after you empty your lungs. You can try the easier one first. After mastering that, you can try the more challenging way.

The third way is to split the breath-holding period in two and place one part after inhalation and the other part after exhalation. In other words, you spend seven seconds inhaling, hold your breath for three seconds, spend seven seconds exhaling, and, finally, hold your breath for another three seconds. This method gives you the opportunity to train at holding your breath after exhalation. Once you are accustomed to this method, you can go to methods one and two described above.

Step 5

If you can breathe comfortably at three cycles per minute, your final goal in this chapter is to reduce it to two cycles per minute, or thirty seconds per cycle. The training process is very similar to that of Step 4. You can figure this out on your own, so I will skip describing the details here.

You may be asking if two cycles per minute is the ultimate goal. No, it is not. The ultimate goal for the martial artist, I think, would be one cycle per minute. In fact, some yoga experts and Zen masters can extend their breathing much longer. My average breathing frequency when I am meditating is about two times per minute. Even though it is a good number, I have not reached the master level yet. My current goal is to reduce it to

one time per minute.

Try the simple exercise described above and see if you can lengthen your breathing cycle. If you are busy and cannot find spare time every day, you can do the breath training while you drive. This will not only train your breathing but, at the same time, also keep you relaxed. As a result, you will be less tired from driving as you exercise slow breathing. If, like me, your hobby is reading books, then this training will go along perfectly with your reading. You will enjoy reading, and your eyes will not get tired as fast as before. If you also have to work in front of a computer for a long time, this exercise will help you with your concentration.

The benefits are almost limitless, and a wonderful thing about breathing exercises is that you can do them almost anytime and anywhere. You have no excuse not to do them. After getting used to this training in your daily life, you can easily implement it in your karate training.

Heartbeat

To me, the greatest benefit I can get from longer breathing is a slower heartbeat. A doctor may tell you that you cannot control the speed or action of your heart, but it is not true. By breathing differently, you can. If you hold your breath, say, for a minute, your heartbeat will increase. On the other hand, if you lengthen your breath, your heartbeat will decrease.
By practicing this closely, you can control the action of your heart, as well as its speed and rhythm.

This ability should be a great benefit if you are an athlete. The average heart rate is sixty to a hundred beats per minute. The goal should be to stay somewhere between fifty and sixty beats per minute. This is not medical advice as I am not a medical doctor, but I am suggesting this because it works for me. Heartbeats differ significantly, depending on various conditions, so the numbers I have mentioned here are only a guideline.

Relaxation

Another benefit to slow, controlled breathing is the total relaxation that goes further than your muscles. You will be able to unconsciously relax your blood vessels, which means they will have a larger diameter, allowing more blood to flow. Increased blood flow to

Deep Breathing Relaxation

your head during meditation will help you if you wish to reach the state of nirvana or total *mu* (無). This is why Zen meditation includes a very slow breathing practice.

Being able to pump more blood through your circulatory system will help you during training, won't it? In addition, after a hard karate training session, you can recuperate faster with relaxed blood vessels. If you have a problem with sleeping after a hard training session in the evening, I recommend that you do slow, controlled breathing down to two breathing cycles per minute. This will slow your heart rate and cause your brain waves to change to alpha (and maybe even down to theta). Then, I guarantee you will get some very restful sleep very quickly. Relaxed blood vessels can also prevent many cases of heart attacks and strokes. Just as you can relax your muscles, you can train to relax your blood vessels. This may be a controversial statement, but I have been practicing this, and I believe in it.

Immune-System Improvement

I guarantee you will have better health with this breathing exercise. Believe

it or not, you can overcome hay-fever and
allergy symptoms. If you suffer from this,
then you need to improve your breathing
as well as your diet (which is another subject to be discussed separately).

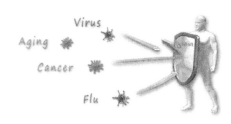

After your exercise, let me hear from you. I would like to know if you feel
better or notice improvement in your karate training. Of course, training in this
for only one day will not have any visible impact, but I am sure you will notice
that this exercise makes you feel better.

Slow down. That is the key to breathing! *Osu!*

I hope my suggestions will help you with your breathing. There are many
other breathing methods and exercises. If you wish to improve further, you can
investigate and find those methods.

CHAPTER EIGHTEEN
第十八章

LOVE
THE ULTIMATE GOAL OF BUDO
愛は武道の究極

I am pretty sure the title of this chapter is at least surprising, maybe unbelievable, and possibly ludicrous to many readers. Hard-core *budoka* (武 道家, 'martial artists') say and believe that *budo* is the art of killing. In fact, I covered this subject in detail in Chapter 5 of this work. If the ultimate goal of *budo* is killing, how can I state that the ultimate goal of *budo* is love in this chapter? These

seemingly contradictory statements, as I explained in chapters 3 and 4, are just opposite sides of the same coin. Nevertheless, this ultimate goal is the biggest secret of *budo*, and this is why I have placed this chapter at the end of this book.

Before I share my thoughts and beliefs on this subject, let's bring out the popular goals of karate training that are commonly shared among *karateka*. The list I will share may not quite match the goals you may have. I am sharing only the most popular ones that I know of. I am also aware that the list is not comprehensive or totally accurate.

The first one is self-defense. Whether you are a man or woman, I am sure being able to defend yourself is very important to you. I suspect many karate practitioners started karate training for this purpose. So, it is very natural to believe that this must be the ultimate goal of karate, and I am sure many people do. Until recently, I also believed this. I would like to come back to this objective later to discuss it further.

By the way, the concept of self-defense itself is an interesting subject. I wrote about it in Chapter 9: "What Is 'Complete' Self-Defense?" of my book *Shotokan Transcendence*. There is also another topic that is very interesting to discuss, as well, which is the question of whether knowing karate really helps in a self-defense situation. Of course, the answer will vary depending on how well you know karate and also on what kind of situation you may be in. Well, this is another subject entirely, so I will get back to the original subject.

The second popular objective of karate training may be health reasons. Practitioners typically attend dojo training two or three times per week. A class is normally between 60 and 90 minutes long. The physical activity guidelines issued by the U.S. Department of Health and Human Services recommend at least 150 minutes per week for adults. So, if you train twice a week at 90 minutes per class or three times a week at 60 minutes per class, you will satisfy the requirement. The required physical activity of mostly moderate and some intense exercises also fits karate training.

So, regular karate training seems to be an excellent way to stay in good health. Ironically, I have met and known hundreds of practitioners who have suffered knee and back problems that seem to have come from karate training. A couple of my karate friends, one in his forties and the other in his sixties, have had to have complete hip-joint replacements. More than a dozen have had to have knee surgery. Well, it is difficult to convince all of those who don't practice karate that karate training is always healthy. We can safely say that karate training itself is healthy. The problem may be practitioners who might have failed to train correctly.

For the physical part, it is easy to see. Typical karate training consists of slow and mild exercise and some fast and rigorous action. This combination is perfect for cardiovascular improvement. In addition, it requires the general movement of all limbs, along with complex, technical, precise movements of the *waza*.

How about the mental part? They say loud yelling, what we call *kiai*, will help relieve your mental stress, even if you are not involved in *kumite*. The effect is greater if your training includes *kumite*, though. Le-gally, you can hit or kick a person. Even though we use the *sundome* system, you can get this satisfaction in a make-believe fighting situation. When you become an expert at it, this will provide you with confidence, which is beneficial to your mental well-being.

The third popular reason that many people start karate training is discipline.

This is an especially popular one, I think, for the parents who send their children to a karate dojo. I have heard many parents telling me that they like the strict discipline that is taught in class. In other words, the children are required to behave throughout the class. The training length for children is typically shorter, maybe 30 to 45 minutes or, at the longest, one hour.

Regardless of class length, children must listen to the commands of the instructor at all times, and, in general, all students must move in unison. This is, at least in Western countries like the U.S., very unusual and rare. Many karate instructors look scary, so kids listen and behave. So, many parents send their kids to learn discipline or to adopt an attitude of listening to authority.

Parents have also told me that they are happy to see that their kids have burned up their energy and gotten some of their frustration out through "aggressive" actions. As a result, their kids are calmer and happier when get home. It is an interesting side effect and probably very legitimate.

Even adult practitioners claim that they practice karate for discipline, even though the meaning of this is somewhat different from when it is used in reference to children. Adults consider a training commitment of two or three times per week to be discipline. Children have no choice as their parents send them to the dojo. Adults, on the other hand, attend the dojo because they wish to do so.

They can have many excuses—such as work, family commitments, and other important adult matters—to skip or even quit training. The training days and times are fixed. They must make a strong commitment and have the dedication to attend week after week for many years. Yes, you must discipline yourself. If you can do this for many years, then other commitments seem to be rather easy.

I am sure there are many other reasons to practice karate. However, finding all of those reasons is not my aim in this chapter, so I will stop this process here. What I need to do is explain why I proposed that mastering love is the ultimate goal of karate training.

Before I get into the explanation, I need to forewarn you that what I write here is my personal belief. For many readers, what you read may sound ridiculous and fabricated. Whether you believe what I present here or not is not important as I am not trying to convince anyone. I am simply presenting my understanding and belief. OK, I needed to tell you this first.

Through karate training, you want to develop true love toward human beings, which is similar to the Christian term *agape* (αγάπη, 'love'). However, it is much more than this. It must be a love not only toward humans but also toward all of nature. Once that is achieved, you will not need to fight anymore. With higher vibrations in your spirit, you can keep yourself in perfect health. Your immune system will be strong and proficient so that you will never get sick. You will be surrounded by similar types of people, and your life will be filled with happiness. This is the ultimate goal I propose.

Even if you excel in your karate technique, without attaining true love, you cannot avoid enemies or ill fate. If your character is rotten rather than pure, this fact will attract similar kinds of people. As they say, birds of a feather flock together. This unavoidably results in conflicts and fights. You may be able to defeat the first enemy, but you will encounter another one, and another one after that. It will be endless.

If you understand the concept of vibrations and frequencies, you will understand what I am trying to explain here and will not think that what I am presenting is totally illogical. Here I need to introduce the solfeggio frequencies, which may not be familiar to all *karateka*. If you happen to favor Gregorian chants, then you may know this term.

What are the solfeggio frequencies? The Nature Healing Society explains them as follows:

The solfeggio frequencies are part of the olden six-tone scale believed to have incorporated sacred music, inclusive of the famous and beautiful Gregorian chants.

The unique tones and chants are found to impart spiritual blessings when they are

THE SOLFEGGIO SCALE
AND CHAKRA HEALING

CROWN CHAKRA - RESET - 936HZ
THIRD EYE - AWAKEN - 852 HZ
THROAT CHAKRA - EXPRESS - 741 HZ
HEART CHAKRA - CONNECT - 639 HZ
SOLAR PLEXUS - LOVE - 528 HZ
SACRAL CHAKRA - RESOLVE - 417 HZ
ROOT CHAKRA - LIBERATE - 396 HZ

played harmoniously. Every solfeggio tone comprises frequencies necessary for balancing energy, keeping the spirit, mind, and body in a perfect form of harmony.

Solfeggio is the use of sol-fa syllables to note scale tones, that is, solmization. Solfeggio is also known as a singing exercise where syllables will be used other than using texts. There exist two types of solfeggio: the movable-do and the fixed-do. (www.naturehealingsociety.com/articles/solfeggio/)

Here are the six main solfeggio frequencies:

- 396 Hz: liberating guilt and fear
- 417 Hz: undoing situations and facilitating change
- 528 Hz: transformation and miracles (DNA repair)
- 639 Hz: connecting/relationships
- 741 Hz: expression/solutions
- 852 Hz: returning to spiritual order

Out of these six frequencies, 528 Hz in particular is considered to be the love frequency and is described as being for transformation and miracles. Believe it or not, it is also classified as a DNA-repair frequency. Isn't that amazing? In music, you will find it very harmonic and beautiful. No wonder it is classified as the DNA-repair and miracle frequency. Here is an image of the love frequency so you can check it out.

Where in your body do you think this vibration comes from? I believe it comes from one of the *tanden* or chakras. There are twelve chakras all together, but there are only seven main ones. Out of these seven, three are popular and well known by martial artists, including *karateka*. Of course, the *seika tanden* (image right) is the most well known among karate practitioners. It is located inside the belly, a little lower than the navel. The *jotanden* (上丹田)

is located between the eyes, near the pineal gland. It is functional for the mental aspects of your life. The love vibration comes from the midsection of the body, or *chutanden*, near the heart.

In many dojo, the importance of the *seika tanden* may be explained and emphasized. Unfortunately, not much, if any, emphasis is placed on the *chutanden* or *jotanden*. But, both are critical and necessary to achieve the ultimate goal of *karatedo*.

Even though the *jotanden* is as important as the other *tanden*, I will not go further with this chakra as I wish to focus on the *chutanden* in this chapter. Many people, including karate instructors, falsely believe that the heart is only a bodily organ used for pumping blood. I believe it is much more than this. What I disclose here may be controversial, but it has been discovered that our heart has its own memory function. It also handles feelings and emits the 528 Hz love frequency.

Here I need to bring up another term that will be unfamiliar to nonscientific readers: *the toroidal energy field of the heart*. According to *Techopedia*, A toroid is

> a doughnut-shaped object with a coil wound around it that is used as an inductor in electronic devices. The shape is described in mathematics as an object or surface generated by revolving a closed plane around an external axis that is parallel to it so it does not intersect; the resulting shape is doughnut-like, and the referred axis is at the very center of the open space. (www.techopedia.com/definition/15036/toroid)

You may not know it, but your heart emits an extremely powerful toroidal energy field (image right). It has actually been measured by scientists. Believe it or not, it can spread out as far as five miles from your heart. In fact, 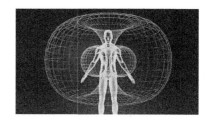 toroidal energy fields exist around everything, including people, the earth, the sun, and the universe. Science has recently shed some light on the fact that what we used to perceive as a human aura is actually real. If you are interested in this subject, read "The Heart's Energy Field" at this URL: https://wellbodymindheartspirit.com/2012/01/11/the-hearts-energy-field/.

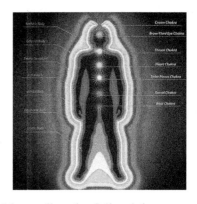

According to the article "The Magnetic Field of the Heart," the human heart can and does affect the earth's electromagnetic field. This is a very interesting subject, and if you are interested in reading the full article on this finding by Dr. Gregg Braden, whom I respect very much, here is the URL to that article: https://schoolofthedeepheart.com/the-magnetic-field-of-the-heart-by-gregg-braden/.

Now that I have emphasized the importance of love in *budo* training, you may be asking, "If you attain ultimate love, will you also attain martial-arts skill at the same time?" In other words, if you have true love, then do you not need to practice any martial arts to defend yourself? True love in Christianity is called *agape*. Maybe a saint has this quality. But, a very religious person may believe he has attained agape, even if he is not at the level of a saint. In that case, if a crazy man attacks him, will he be saved because he has agape? Unfortunately, I do not think that is the case. Then, why do I say that the ultimate goal of martial arts is love?

Here is a motto from the Japanese martial arts that you may already know: *shingitai* (心技体). If you understand this, then you will understand what I am proposing in this chapter. As you may already know, we are supposed to master these three conditions or areas in order to master any Japanese art, which, of course, includes *budo*.

The Japanese word *shin* (心) literally means 'heart'. It also means 'feelings', 'psyche', etc. It is similar to 'mind' and 'thought' and yet quite different. The words *mind* and *thought* refer to things that come from the brain, while *shin* comes from the heart. We have to train our mind and have a calm and peaceful mindset. This is placed at the top of the list as it is the most valuable because it is the hardest to achieve. But, at the same time, you cannot achieve the ultimate essence of martial arts by having a peaceful mind alone. You must train in a martial art such as karate to develop the proper skill set with your body in order to achieve this. Before we dig more deeply into the *shin* category, let's cover the other two as they are easier for us to understand.

Gi (技) means 'technique' or 'method'. So, you can easily understand that you must learn and master the techniques of the martial arts or the method of fighting. This is exactly what we do in our dojo. We repeat *kihon* many times. We are supposed to spend three years mastering one *kata*. We also learn how to fight using the basics and techniques found in the *kata*. This is called *kumite*.

If you are practicing any style of karate, you are engaged in all of these aspects of training. So, to excel in karate, we all agree that we must master the karate techniques.

In addition to this, you must also work on *tai* (体), which means 'body'. This one is also easy to understand. If our body is weak, then you cannot fight. For instance, if you are weak, you can hit your opponent but cause little damage. It is obvious that you will not be able to defend yourself.

Even if you are very strong, what if you are extremely slow? This happens with bulky musclemen. A bodybuilder may look tough and seem like an excellent fighter, but he may be too slow to fight a smaller man with great fighting skill. So, you need to be fast, as well.

In addition to power and speed, flexibility and balance are also required. If your joints are too tight and inflexible, naturally, your fighting ability will suffer. For instance, if you cannot get your leg up higher than knee level, would you not consider your kicking ability to be poor? Of course you would!

Then, why include balance? If you understand the kinesiology of your body, you can easily see that without good balance, producing excellent kicks becomes difficult. As you know, kicking requires standing on one leg during the process. The duration of a kick is very short, so you may not realize that you need to work on your balance. Believe me, there is a huge difference between a kick (or even a punch) that comes from poor balance and one that comes from a well-balanced stance and posture. I am not referring to a difference only in power but also in the overall effect, including distance, angle, posture, follow-up, etc.

Regardless, we agree that we need to work on our body, and most of us know how to do that. Your body is something you can see and use all the time. Though training and exercise may be challenging, you know the goals. In addition, you can easily see your level of achievement. If you can only do ten sit-ups, you can set your goal at fifty, one hundred, etc. If you cannot do the splits, you can start working on stretching exercises so that one day you can do the full splits and touch your forehead to the floor. If you do these exercises diligently, you can achieve your goals, no matter how young or old you may be.

So, we agree that we must excel in technique and skill as well as in strength and ability. That was not too difficult. Then, we need to look at the first item, *shin*. This is your heart, your feelings, your mind. What does this mean in relation to the martial arts? There are a few things that are covered by this character. When we use the term *mind*, many people may think that the mind is controlled by our brain. However, martial-arts experts described it with the character for 'heart'. So, let's look at the feelings and state of mind that come from your heart or guts.

First of all, the feeling of fear is closely associated with life-or-death situations. We agree that a true martial artist must overcome fear. You will be a coward if you lack guts or have a weak heart. In addition to fear, you may feel nervousness, impatience, irritation, frustration, etc. In other words, you may experience an unbalanced or unstable mindset. These feelings will not help you in a critical situation. You may move too soon or too late. You may make mistakes. Yes, you will not be able to think or act properly. Thus, you must learn how to keep a peaceful and steady mind. This is to control your mind or heart, but how do you do it?

When it comes to your body, you can exercise and practice to strengthen it and improve your skill. You can easily see how to do that. Your mind, on the other hand, is quite different. Can you easily figure out how to train and strengthen your mind? The samurai had the same challenge. Many tried to do it by putting themselves through rigorous train-  ing. Some tried Zen and meditation. A few crazy ones, I heard, slept with a sword hanging from the ceiling above their face to overcome their fear. Many samurai, when they would wake up in the morning, would recite in their mind, or sometimes aloud, that this was their last day alive. They tried to avoid wanting to survive or live until the next day. Once you can convince yourself that you are going to die today, then there will be nothing that can scare you.

For the samurai, that was probably a practical solution as they faced death very frequently. However, unless you are a soldier or a law enforcement officer, this kind of approach may not be too practical. Regardless, attaining a permanent calm and a peaceful mind is extremely difficult even for us. When the car next to you cuts you off abruptly, do you not get upset? If you are in line at the post office, and the line does not progress for a long time, do you not become impatient? When you are in bed late at night and hear a loud banging sound in the kitchen when no one is supposed to be there, how do you feel? How about if the airplane you are traveling on gets into strong turbulence and, all of a sudden, starts to dive sharply? Will you not be scared? It is not easy to keep our mind calm and peaceful in these situations. I hope you understand why *shin* is listed at the top of the three elements of achievement for master martial artists.

So, why am I proposing that love is the ultimate goal? As you know, there are many levels and kinds of love in this world. You are familiar with the feelings between parents and their children. You also experience falling in love with your boyfriend or girlfriend. You may feel love toward not only your best friends but also your close friends. If you have a dog or cat, I am sure you love your pet. Well, these are people and other living things around you. You can also love your job or your interests. It could be a hobby, such as fishing, fixing your car, cooking, knitting, playing golf, etc. I am sure that many of you will say, "I love karate." You could expand your love even further to people who have suffered a disaster in a foreign country.

I am sure you can find other things that you can love. At the same time, not too many people would say, "I love my enemy." Earlier I brought up the Christian concept of agape. If you happen to attain this, you are supposed to be able to love even your enemy.

As a martial artist, I am not sure if I can love my enemy, but it might be possible to develop or control my emotions so that I would not hate that person. Instead, I would feel sad and sorry to see him trying to harm me. I could possibly feel this way without hating him as a person. If he attacked me, I would defend myself but without any negative feelings. My feelings would be, I suspect, neutral. I would imagine that level must be filled with benevolence and compassion. If I could reach that level, then my feelings would be calm and peaceful, even when facing my enemy.

Yes, fear is a difficult challenge to a martial artist. At the same time, there are many other negative feelings that a karate practitioner must overcome. For instance, say, if you were a karate instructor, and you happened to have a young student who had an attention deficit. Even if you knew the student had a handicap, would you be able to maintain your patience all the time? I have had this very experience, and it was very difficult. It taught me how to be patient.

If you had to examine your son or daughter for a *dan* rank, could you be totally fair and honest in your judgment? Do you give examinations often to make money? Do you make adjustments to your training to make it easier for fear that some would otherwise quit? How about your *dan* rank? I am sure you did not purchase a *dan* diploma from a not-so-reputable organization, but have you ever felt that temptation? Do you compete in tournaments for the purpose of collecting medals instead of learning or improving your karate? I can go on with many other not-so-honorable things that we must fight against.

Well, it is easy to blame those who are cowardly or dishonest. You can despise or disrespect those who have a weak heart. But, can you really? Are we perfect ourselves? No, we are not. In fact, we all know that it is extremely difficult for anyone to develop strong morals and become fully brave. To conquer those challenges, the answer seems to be love.

Interestingly, Albert Einstein (1879–1955), one of the greatest physicists of all time, said that there was an extremely powerful force in the universe. He stated that the science of his time had not found a formal ex-

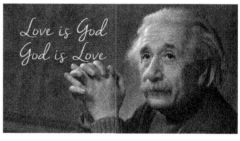

planation and is said to have concluded, "This universal force is LOVE." I found his conclusion extremely interesting and enlightening. According to his theory, we can reach or be with God when we discover love. If we can do this, there is nothing to be afraid of.

Then, how can we find love? They say that worldly things decrease when you give them away, while love increases when you give it away. This may be a great hint. I will start sharing and giving more of my love and care to as many people as I can. What are you willing to do?

EPILOGUE
エピローグ

EINSTEIN'S LETTER TO HIS DAUGHTER
アインシュタイン、娘への手紙

I learned about this letter from my karate friend, Rick Davies, in Blooming-
dale, Michigan. I want to thank him
for the information.

In the late 1980s, Albert Einstein's
daughter Lieserl supposedly donated
1400 letters that were written by him to the Hebrew University. For some unknown reason, Einstein, again, supposedly asked her not to publish the contents
until two decades after his death, so she waited until the eighties to disclose them.

I will attach the content of the letter that was supposedly addressed to his
daughter below.

When I proposed the theory of relativity, very few understood me, and what I will
reveal now to transmit to mankind will also collide with the misunderstanding and
prejudice in the world.

I ask you to guard the letters as long as necessary, years, decades, until society is
advanced enough to accept what I will explain below.

There is an extremely powerful force that, so far, science has not found a formal
explanation to. It is a force that includes and governs all others, and is even behind
any phenomenon operating in the universe and has not yet been identified by us.

This universal force is LOVE.

When scientists looked for a unified theory of the universe, they forgot the most
powerful unseen force.

Love is Light that enlightens those who give and receive it.

Love is gravity, because it makes some people feel attracted to others.

Love is power, because it multiplies the best we have, and allows humanity not
to be extinguished in their blind selfishness. Love unfolds and reveals.

For love we live and die.

Love is God and God is Love.

This force explains everything and gives meaning to life. This is the variable
that we have ignored for too long, maybe because we are afraid of love because it is
the only energy in the universe that man has not learned to drive at will.

To give visibility to love, I made a simple substitution in my most famous equa-
tion.

If instead of $E=mc^2$, we accept that the energy to heal the world can be obtained through love multiplied by the speed of light squared, we arrive at the conclusion that love is the most powerful force there is, because it has no limits.

After the failure of humanity in the use and control of the other forces of the universe that have turned against us, it is urgent that we nourish ourselves with another kind of energy.

If we want our species to survive, if we are to find meaning in life, if we want to save the world and every sentient being that inhabits it, love is the one and only answer.

Perhaps we are not yet ready to make a bomb of love, a device powerful enough to entirely destroy the hate, selfishness and greed that devastate the planet.

However, each individual carries within them a small but powerful generator of love whose energy is waiting to be released.

When we learn to give and receive this universal energy, dear Lieserl, we will have affirmed that love conquers all, is able to transcend everything and anything, because love is the quintessence of life.

I deeply regret not having been able to express what is in my heart, which has quietly beaten for you all my life. Maybe it's too late to apologize, but as time is relative, I need to tell you that I love you and thanks to you I have reached the ultimate answer!

Your father,

Albert Einstein

Now, this is a beautiful letter, and it really touched my heart strongly. This s why I decided to add it to this book. At the same time, I also learned later that many people doubt the authenticity of this letter. I will bring up two sites where I obtained reasons for the doubt.

One source is Snopes (www.snopes.com/fact-check/einstein-universal-orce/), which is the Internet's definitive fact-checking resource site. They gave he letter a rating of "False," and here are some of the reasons they reached this conclusion:

- According to their research, his daughter Lieserl was born in 1902. She was supposedly born with a severe mental handicap and was possibly blind.
- Lieserl caught scarlet fever in 1903 and is assumed to have died that year at the age of twenty-one months. This was assumed to be the case because there is no mention of her by Einstein or his wife after that year.
- This letter is unlike any other writings by Einstein in tone and content.
- Several distinctive phrases—I assume one is "Love is God and God is love" —fail to match any other existing papers or writings.

Snopes inferred that someone was trying to get readers to pay attention to the message by attributing it to a well-known, respected figure such as Einstein. If it was not written by him, then this sounds very possible.

The other source I'll share here is *HuffPost* (www.huffpost.com/entry/the-truth-behind-einsteins-letter-on-the-universal-force-of-love_b_7949032), an American liberal news aggregator and blog site. *HuffPost* claims, after intensive research, that this letter is a fabrication and is falsely attributed to Einstein in an attempt to legitimize its words and messages. Here are some reasons they came to this conclusion:

- Einstein's daughter Lieserl was very little known until 1986; thus, she might not be the most reliable source.
- They also believe Lieserl was born with a mental handicap and that she died of scarlet fever in 1903. Another possibility they pointed out was that she could have been put up for adoption, which is why she is not mentioned after 1903.
- They cited a statement by Diana Kormos-Buchwald, a professor of physics and the history of science at Caltech. She claimed the letter was not

written by Einstein because the person who donated the 1400 letters to the Hebrew University was not Lieserl. It was his stepdaughter Margot.

For these reasons, *HuffPost* concluded that this letter was not written by Einstein. Even though I understand why they came to this conclusion, I do not understand why they called the letter a fabrication. The letter itself can easily be genuine, even if it was not written by a world-renowned physicist.

I totally understand why these researchers from these two sites concluded that this letter might not have been written by Einstein. On the other hand, I point out that the reasons stated above are all circumstantial. I consider the degree of conclusiveness to be about ninety percent. In other words, this leaves a small, ten-percent chance that it was written by him.

If Einstein had no daughter, then I would say this would be one-hundred-percent proof that it was a fabrication. If Einstein himself wrote somewhere that he did not write this letter, then that would be one-hundred-percent proof. But, of course, we do not have such a letter as he passed before this letter became public.

If it was indeed written by him, we can possibly explain why he wrote to his daughter Lieserl, who might have died at the age of two. Since the content is not very scientific and is very different from all of the writings he had done in the past, he could have decided to share this incredible idea with a dead daughter. Since she was in heaven, he believed that she would understand it. Of course, this is only a wild guess of mine.

Regardless of who, in fact, wrote this beautiful letter, I believe the core essence exists. Even though I am not a physicist or a scientist, I can feel with my heart that the core message is true and correct.

I am not trying to convince anyone that this letter was actually written by Einstein. I listed two sites in order to check into those who believe it was fabricated. All I can say is that only God knows. It is totally up to you to decide whether you believe this letter is genuine or fabricated. I only ask you to read it with your heart.

Even if this is a fabrication, the question of who is really behind this beautiful letter about the "universal force" of love is left unanswered. Yes, it is still a big mystery. This is one of the reasons this letter befits this book.

Printed in Great Britain
by Amazon

11963462R00153